INSPIRITED

From the Annals of Annah

SHEILA ANNETTE SWIFT

ISBN: 1502418290
ISBN 13: 9781502418296
Library of Congress Control Number: 2014916857
CreateSpace Independent Publishing Platform
North Charleston, South Carolina

INSPIRITED
(A true story from the Annals of Annah)

Sheila Annette Swift

DISCLAIMER
I have tried to recreate events, locales and conversations from my memories of them. In order to maintain their anonymity, in all instances, I have changed the names of individuals, and places. I have changed some identifying characteristics and details such as physical properties, occupations and places of residence.

Dedication.....

I dedicate this book to my loving family
for having the patience for me to heal on my own terms,
in my own time.
They are my driving force, my every breath, my reason for living.
They define, for me, unconditional love.
Without their love, support and family dynamic,
I would not be alive today to tell my story.

Amanda, Melissa, Erika & Kristina

A MEKS...forever

ACKNOWLEDGEMENTS.....

Thank you friends, family, and everyone else
who has touched my life.
You have all shaped who I am,
helped me grow as a person,
and presented me with opportunities and experiences
that enriched my life with invaluable lessons.

A special thanks to William Joseph for always
being there for me and encouraging
me in every way.

Jessica Capers for reading my book on
her phone, quite a feat I must say!

Jack (Bloopyguy) for being a great men-
tor and awesome friend.

Mike Valentino (www.editor-ghostwriter.com)
for a job well done in editing my book and
helping me rewrite a difficult chapter.

Michele Hunter (Publisher Services,
www.isbn-us.com)for her independent review.

CreateSpace for their professional formatting
and cover design.

TABLE OF CONTENTS

PROLOGUE

What if I was to tell you a story that would defy everything you were brought up to believe? Would you question your beliefs or defend them? We all know there is a higher being, but we still have questions that go unanswered; yet we still believe. Are we just creatures of habit, afraid to go against the tried and true? Do we just go through the motions because that's what is expected of us?

Annah was just like you until her day of enlightenment. She doesn't want anyone to change their beliefs, just to be open to what she experienced. This story is like no other and Annah will tell you, she would never have believed it if she hadn't lived through it herself.

She was scared and knew deep in her soul someone or something was with her. Frightened and alone, she had nowhere to go and no one to talk to. She had entered a dark, desolate place. Her world had become very still. It was as if all animate objects became frozen in time and the sound of silence became frightfully deafening.

Annah had often thought that we are all put on this earth as angels or guardians of goodness but deep within us, the devil resides, waiting for the chance to rear its ugly head and dominate humanity. It is the greed, control and power that create recession and destruction so it is within our power to avert this by staying true to ourselves.

We must respect all of mankind and appreciate the natural elements and beautiful habitat we were given. We are all tested and tempted every day but some are too weak to abstain from grievous acts that cause others misery, desolation and, in some cases, fatal despair. The unfortunate truth in our ever deteriorating society is that we have been cultivated to believe that glamour and glory sparkle more than pain and suffering.

We don't realize the errors in our paths until our day of reckoning, which could be as soon as tomorrow. Every moment, every act, every notion determines our fate and ultimately our destiny....so heed this warning and choose your actions wisely.

Know also that wisdom is like honey for you:
If you find it, there is a future hope for you,
and your hope will not be cut off.

Do not lurk like a thief near the house of the righteous,
do not plunder their dwelling place;
for though the righteous fall seven times, they rise again,
but the wicked stumble when calamity strikes.

Do not gloat when your enemy falls;
when they stumble, do not let your heart rejoice,
or the LORD will see and disapprove
and turn his wrath away from them.

Do not fret because of evildoers
or be envious of the wicked,
for the evildoer has no future hope,
and the lamp of the wicked will be snuffed out.

Fear the LORD and the king, my son,
and do not join with rebellious officials,
for those two will send sudden destruction on them,
and who knows what calamities they can bring?

~Proverbs 24:14-22

XIII

IN THE BEGINNING

In court her divorce was finalized around three o'clock in the afternoon just as her commuter plane approached Bradley International. The landing gear abruptly chirped against the asphalt runway, tousling the passengers gently about before steadying. She hadn't even noticed they had landed. Her thoughts were off in the future, envisioning her new life as a free and single woman.

Savannah, or Annah (her girlhood nickname), was now free to explore and expand as a person; to realize the dreams she had neatly packed away years ago; to finally put herself and her needs first. After twenty-two years of marriage, most of which had been reduced to cohabitation, it was apparent they had lost any semblance of the youthful passion that had brought them together. As time passed, a day didn't go by that they didn't verbally demoralize one another.

Annah's ex-husband, Jack, couldn't believe her trip took precedence over hearing the judge proclaim the dissolution of their marriage. Annah, on the other hand, couldn't understand why she would have gone to court. They were already divorced on paper, the court proceeding was just a formality. In hindsight, maybe it was a deliberate attempt on her part to push that final button.

Annah and Jack had four beautiful daughters who were gifts from heaven. From the moment they were born, they became the center of Annah's universe—her love for them would never be eclipsed…by anyone. Jack soon became envious. He wanted the same amount of time, attention, and affection the girls were getting and had no problem expressing his selfish displeasure. She knew many guys felt that way, but they eventually outgrew it.

So with such a dysfunctional marriage, why did they have so many children? Maybe it felt like the natural evolutionary order of life, or maybe it filled an emotional void by offering and receiving love and companionship on a different level. They had dated for a little over five years when they got married, at the tender age of twenty, which somewhat accounts for the naiveté of not knowing what forever meant, let alone true love. Young, innocent and freewheeling, they dove headfirst into a pool of delusive idealizations of happily ever after, holding on to the safety net that love conquers all.

For all intents and purposes, however, they played their parts well. They were the perfect couple and family, attending social gatherings together, going to dinner as a family, vacationing together—the American dream. She was determined not to dwell on the past. Onward and upward was her mantra.

The only downside of her newly acquired single status was the dilemma of all single Moms. She now had to juggle the responsibilities of her full-time job, running the kids to their activities, and single handedly maintaining the household, so her 'spare time' soon evaporated.

Needless to say, when Annah was asked to travel for business, she readily accepted; it was a fun and sometimes necessary diversion. Each trip offered a new experience; a different culture, charming, charismatic people, and experimenting with the local, sometimes exotic, cuisine—she had actually tried fried alligator bites and frog legs in Louisiana, both in the stratosphere of her comfort zone.

Even though things got a little hectic, freedom suited her. She was able to come and go without anyone's permission, make her own decisions without prior approval, and most importantly, she was able to make mistakes without worrying about repercussions.

Yet Annah came to realize there was something missing. She somehow didn't feel complete. And the missing element, to her surprise, was having a man in her life—she missed having a companion. And now that summer had officially begun, Annah yearned for a worthy consort to share long walks with, to dine with in quaint little restaurants while sipping a good Merlot, to sit under the stars with while effortlessly talking about anything and everything. But mostly, she wanted someone with whom to share intimate and passionate nights.

After about three months of navigating the *singles scene* as a mere spectator, she decided to aggressively put herself out there as single and available.

But having been married for so many years, she was intimidated and basically unversed on modern dating etiquette. And because she is such a private person, she felt uncomfortably exposed creating a dating profile where perfect strangers could view her picture, hobbies, likes, dislikes and personality traits. She was old-school and believed a viable suitor should go through the painstaking task of wooing her and winning her heart. She knew her approach to dating was quite archaic, but it didn't matter, she wasn't going to change her style. So after careful consideration, she decided to go a more traditional, safer route.

That being said, she got the word out to friends that she was *on the prowl*, hoping it would circulate and reach her target audience. Well, it did circulate. In less than a week she received a call from Maddie, a friend of nearly fifteen years. Maddie knew of a single guy who was going through a divorce, and whose criterion was similar to Annah's. He was looking for a companion, a person to hang out with, possibly leading to something deeper and more meaningful later on down the road.

Annah agreed to the blind date but approached it reservedly and guarded knowing she shouldn't expect too much. She wanted to be herself—confident, witty, sincere and fun-loving. She didn't broadcast her intentions to her daughters fearing they would think it was too soon and she knew, even though it was never expressed, they secretly hoped Mom and Dad would someday get back together. Annah didn't have the heart to burst their bubble.

Exactly one week later, it was time to put Maddie's match making skills to the test. It wasn't that Annah didn't trust Maddie's judgment; it was just that everyone's tastes are different. Annah's biggest fear, however, was that her blind date wouldn't even show up, or worse, if he did, would he be on the short list of dating rejects? She wrote off her apprehensiveness as being the newest and most inexperienced member of the dating world.

It was one hour till show time and Annah couldn't decide how she was going to dress to impress. Her work clothes would have made her look stiff, formal, not fun loving and her shorts and halter probably would have gotten her one terrific date, but nothing more. So, after careful consideration, she finally came to the conclusion that she should just stay true to herself, and to her initial goal of just having fun. So the outfit of choice—jeans, peasant top and flip flops.

A nearby country club was the selected venue for their introduction. Annah walked to the entrance where she waited for Maddie, hoping she would be along soon. Even though the sun was sinking behind the sparkling green golf course, the residual heat lingered on. Sweat beads began to multiply on her forehead which joined together and streamed down her face, while the unforgivable, albeit typical summer humidity decided to restyle her perfectly styled hair.

When Maddie arrived a few minutes later, they walked in together and slowly made their way around the rectangular bar that served as the centerpiece of the room. Annah let Maddie lead the way knowing she would find strategic seating that would enable peripheral viewing. The Lounge, as it was called, was quite busy, a lively entertainment hub with dining tables, a pool table, poker tables and a makeshift stage where a local band was performing.

Never having been there before, Annah gazed around the room with the wide-eyed curiosity of a child in a toy store—at least that's how she hoped it appeared. In all honestly, she was hoping in the scope of her gaze, to catch a glimpse of the mystery man.

From the immediate considerations, none of whom were overly appealing, she had forgotten the multitude of male variations that were out there. One was tall with dark hair and reasonably attractive, but seemed unapproachable; another was short and balding and heckled loudly for obvious attention; while another had his shirt unbuttoned so far down it barely covered his hairy beer belly. It didn't take long for her to come to the conclusion that the 'blind' in blind dates suck. There were too many unknown factors.

While waiting for their beer to arrive, Annah casually panned the room one more time. But unfortunately, out of the many men scattered throughout, not one caught her eye. The manhunt was already depressing, so she played catch up with Maddie instead. They laughed and reminisced, but all the while Annah was distracted by thoughts that maybe he was discreetly checking her out as well, and was just as curious about her looks. And that's when she realized that maybe she wasn't his type, or maybe she didn't have what he was looking for. Annah became so tangled in her own insecurities that she wasn't contributing much to the conversation that had already ended moments earlier.

Out of sheer angst, she pulled Maddie in close and whispered, "Which one is he? Could you point him out?"

Maddie, who had already engaged in another conversation, giggled and rested her hand on the bar lifting only her index finger to point in his direction.

"He's the one in the white shirt."

He was on the other side of the room playing poker with five other men, who fortunately had on different colored shirts. Annah nonchalantly tilted her head down and slyly peered at him. Feeling foolish about taking such an adolescent approach, she justified it by thinking an outright stare would have been too conspicuous. She was more so wanting to see if he was sneaking in a peek at her, but not once did he even so much as glance in her direction.

She managed to inventory his physical appearance. He must have been a solid five foot eleven, which was just right for her petite five foot frame. The way his broad shoulders and defined chest filled out his polo shirt, suggested the scale tipped in favor of athleticism. Overall, his presence advocated a sense of refinement, giving Annah the impression that appearance while important was not obsessive—which was a major plus in her book. Admittedly, he wasn't anyone she would have picked out of a dating line-up. But as far as blind dates go, he wasn't bad at all.

She took note that he was winning hand after hand. He was actually very good, but his casual cockiness suggested that maybe he knew it. After about a half hour, waiting anxiously, Annah urged Maddie to remind him that they were there.

Maddie agrees and calls his cell phone.

"Are you going to come over and meet your blind date or play cards all night?" she quips.

Annah watched as he pushed all his chips to the center of the table, bluffing his way through a pathetic pair of nines, ultimately losing everything. After excusing himself from the table, he walked directly to the bar across from where they sat, to refill his draft. He took a sip, which Annah thought was a sadistic way to prolong the agony; he then casually worked his way over to them.

Finally I get to meet him!

She secretly hoped the moment would unfold like she'd seen in several movies and read in numerous romance novels.

The lights dimmed, wafting cigar smoke hovered over the bar, conversations become muffled and the spotlight shone on the two. When their eyes met, they both knew fate had brought them there. With every passing moment, their adoration grew. He was tall, dark and exceptionally handsome, even more so than Adonis himself. Who was this stranger that I was to spend the rest of my life with?

Annah was irrefutably the poster child for hopeless romantics!

In the lagging moments before his arrival, she silently rehearsed everything Maddie had told her about him. His name is Lance; he's in the process of divorcing his second wife; and he lives in a neighboring town with his first wife, (bizarre but true), and mother of three of his children.

"Well, here goes nothing!" Annah felt her body temperature raise a few degrees.

Maddie gave Lance a 'great to see you' hug before the introductions.

"Lance, this is my good friend, Annah."

Maddie continues, "Annah, Lance."

Right away Annah could tell that Lance was more shy and reserved than he had been with his fellow poker players. She immediately sensed a special quality about him and she wanted to get to know him better. So after a drink or three, Annah suggested moving to a quieter area so they could talk without having to shout. They moved to a bistro table by the full length windows facing the back nine of the illuminated golf course. There they got on very well, laughing, joking and sharing quirky stories with no awkward pauses or uncomfortably quiet moments—it felt so natural. They certainly enjoyed each other's company.

Then suddenly, as if the clock struck midnight, Lance announced he was calling it a night. Was the fairy tale prince going to turn into a pumpkin? Without so much as a handshake, he brought his empty mug to the bar and broadcast to the entire inebriated crowd that he was leaving due to a prior commitment he had early the next morning. He waved to Annah from across the room, said good-bye to everyone; then off he went.

Disappointed by her first dating experience since the divorce, Annah couldn't help but wonder if she had done something wrong, said something improper or offensive, or was she just delusional in thinking that Lance was as enamored by her as she was by him. Had she assessed the date differently, thinking it went well when in his mind it hadn't?

"Wow! He didn't even ask for my phone number."

"And no kiss goodnight...what the hell?"

She couldn't help but feel put off. It's not that she expected the first guy she met to be attracted to her, she had just hoped for a great 'get to know each other' evening and anticipated a much better ending. But rather than showing her scorn, she said her goodbyes and left as well.

The next day, Annah was awakened by the obnoxious ring of her cell phone; the generic tone that she never got around to changing since she bought it over a year ago. It was Maddie asking how her night went. Annah enthusiastically expressed the awesomeness of the first couple of hours—then her tone eclipsed, relating Lance's not so congenial farewell.

Maddie offered her apologies for Lance, assuring Annah that he meant no harm or disrespect. In fact, Lance had such a great time he asked Maddie for Annah's number.

After an extended pause, Maddie asks, "Are you there?"

"Yea, yea I'm here. I'm just a little confused, but elated at the same time."

It was that old-fashioned approach that any hopeless romantic would swoon over. Annah was very moved by this humbling overture. It was charming, and something she wasn't used to, so it touched her heart in a very profound way.

"Yes, give him my number. I would like to see him again, and Maddie, thank you for everything."

Later that night, the much anticipated call came in. Their conversation, at first, had no life; only the ordinary pleasantries were exchanged. However, as much as she tried, Annah couldn't get past the way he had left the country club. She found herself waiting for the opportune moment to, nonchalantly, bring it up. It was important for her to be honest and forthright, at the start, if anything were to be created between them in the future. But before Annah had the chance, Lance offered a sincere explanation for his rather capricious departure the night before.

With admirable innocence, he explained, "About last night…I'm sorry for leaving so abruptly. As soon as you walked through the door, I felt the butterflies stirring in my stomach. I mean, look at you, you're beautiful. Never in my wildest dreams would I have imagined a guy like me being with a girl like you."

Her heart amorously fluttered and joyful tears welled up in her eyes. His honesty was so refreshing. She knew, at that very moment, there was something tender, wholesome, and diversely unique about this man—definitely a man worth holding onto. In the few minutes they conversed, she had already sensed a loving, caring, and deeply romantic relationship.

Once the proverbial layer of ice was broken, they continued their lighthearted banter from the night before. Time became a dimension in which they remained playfully engaged until the wee hours of the morning, at which point Annah's involuntary exhaustion got the better of her. But before she let him hang up, he had to promise to call the next day to make plans for their first 'official date'.

Annah clutched her pillow, snuggled her comforter, and imagined the missing component of Lance's arms wrapped around her. She had never believed in love at first sight, but Lance was a game changer. It was as if an angel was watching over her and delivered the one thing she longed for—a loving companion.

It wasn't like Annah to dive in foreign waters without testing it first, so with a healthy dose of realism she reminded herself to take it one step at a time. Her innate wisdom was always a source of solid guidance, and she felt inclined to listen. After all, she had them married and living happily ever after, after just one phone call. But, truth be told, she did feel something she hadn't felt in a long time, and it was wonderful.

ANNAH AND LANCE

Over the next several days, Annah was consumed by a sense that she was given a new lease on love. A new chapter had begun for which she was grateful and all too ready to begin. It has often been said that when one door closes, another opens. Annah had enthusiastically become the latest advocate of this old adage.

Annah's entire demeanor had risen to positive new heights, a bright new life had awakened inside her and she definitely embraced it. Laughter and jocularity became an integral part of her daily repertoire, and she captured a brighter overall optimism to life. Everything was falling into its perfect place. Her once choppy, restless ocean had become a calm, settled sea.

It was eight-thirty sharp when Annah's phone lit up, eagerly displaying Lance's number. She didn't want to appear overly anxious, so she fidgeted through the first three rings. Then, summoning her most alluring voice, she answers, "Hello!"

"Well hello there!"

With a grin in his voice he says, "I wasn't sure you were going to answer when you saw my name come up."

Annah, usually the master of quick-witted comebacks, suddenly finds herself at a loss for words. She wanted to tell him how her stomach did somersaults when his name came up on her phone, and that his call was the highlight of her day, but knew it may have been misconstrued as sounding pathetically love struck.

She hesitates before asserting, "Of course I would answer. I enjoy talking to you."

He quickly professes, "So do I! I mean, I enjoy talking to you as well."

Annah was hoping, amidst their joviality, he would ask her out on their first official date. But between the amusing anecdotes, parenthood stories, and war stories from his marriages, it seemed like it was the furthest thing from his mind. Annah was becoming discouraged. Their conversation was coming to a close and no mention of getting together. This is when she decides to employ her clever guile and drops a not so subtle hint.

"So Lance, what are you doing Friday night?"

"Well" says Lance, "Funny you should ask!"

"I was going to ask if you wanted hang out."

The orchestra was finally playing her song.

Lance suggests they meet at his house and maybe watch a movie, go out for ice cream, or take a leisurely walk through his neighborhood. This wasn't exactly the rendezvous she had in mind, but liked the thought of a more intimate setting. They exchanged email addresses before saying good night.

The next few days ambled along, so you can imagine Annah's relief when Friday rolled around, which embarked on a smooth and copacetic note—full of great expectations. When she got to work, she methodically began her daily routine. She brewed the community pot of coffee, prepped her work station, prioritized her workload for the day, poured her first of many cups of coffee, and booted up her computer. Settling back in her ergonomically correct chair, she began her next ritual of reading and responding to emails.

There was an email from Lance sitting in her inbox. This one she opens right away.

"Good morning, beautiful! Hope you have a great day!"

He must have written it from home, before he left for work. She immediately responded wishing him a great day, then took it up a notch and added how much she was looking forward to their date. Her intent was to keep the email stream running all day, which it did.

At five o'clock sharp, Annah headed out, wishing everyone a great weekend. Earlier in the day, she had decided it was going to be a pizza night for the kids, to free up time to get ready. Her girls would get picked up by their dad at seven and she would head out around eight. That would leave plenty of time to shake off any last minute nerves.

Everything was going according to plan until Annah pulled up at Lance's house. Several cars filled his driveway and lined the street. Could she have gotten the time wrong, or written down the wrong address? That last thing she wanted to do was walk up to the wrong house, only to find out later he was watching the entire time. She finds a place to park and calls him from her car.

"Lance? It's me, Annah. I think I'm at the right house, but it looks like you're having a party," she jokes.

"I'm sure you're at the right house. A few of the guys showed up, unexpectedly, to play poker. I honestly thought we'd be done by now. Just come in, we're in the basement."

Her first thought was, "How and why did he allow this to happen?"

She bit her lip, clenched her fist, and fought to not appear annoyed. It had even crossed her mind to turn around and go home, but she didn't want to appear childish.

"Quite honestly, I don't feel comfortable just letting myself in. Will you please meet me at the door?"

"Of course, I'll be right there!"

Annah followed Lance to the basement where he offered her a seat and a cold drink before returning to the card table to resume his game. It was in a remote corner of the room, which was off-putting, but at that point she considered it par for the already disastrous course the night had taken on.

Leaving her alone wasn't in his best interest. It only compounded her agitation. She began to silently gripe about every little thing, beginning with his underde-veloped etiquette because she wasn't introduced to his poker pals, the disarray of his cluttered basement that was partially finished with shag carpeting and paneling, circa 1970, and the icing on the cake was the offensive, rancid odor that slapped her in the face and took up residence in her clothes from the moment she walked in the front door—he no doubt had a cat or many.

This was not the romantic encounter she had hoped for. She was taken aback by his disregard of her feelings. He misread her good nature and felt she would be okay with watching them play, but had underestimated the power of boredom. After a couple of rounds, Annah decided enough was enough and gestured for Lance to come over.

As much as she wanted to blurt out how she genuinely felt, she knew it would have been too abrasive, something she would probably regret later. So she decided on a more civil approach. She whispered to him, "I'm gonna head out. Work was rough today and I'm extremely tired." He apologized for the way the night turned out, which to Annah seemed like water under the bridge at that point.

Lance walked her to her car, making sure to open the door like a true gentleman. He assured Annah, "The next date will be lady's choice. I will call you tomorrow—promise!" They exchanged good nights, but once again, no good night kiss—not even a hug.

She watched him go back inside before pulling away. It was only a short ride home, but in that time, she wondered whether this person she staked claim to deserved her devout consideration. The sparkling, undiscovered gem she had seen in the beginning had become a crude and unrefined rhinestone. But amidst all the haze that surrounded this budding romance was an enigmatic man who had her entranced by his unsophisticated, muddled charm.

Annah entered her dark and desolate home, using the LED display from the cable box as her only source of illumination. It brightly reported that the evening was still young, 10:11 p.m.

"Wow!" she thought. "I bet that was the shortest date in modern history!"

But something about that time had her reaching far behind its measurement. The time was more of an anomaly that, as of late, was appearing several times in her life. This phenomenon, referred to as a 'repeating number pattern' amuses most people, but others search for its hidden meaning. Annah had read somewhere that the universe sends these as signs, usually correlating to something that has happened or is destined to happen in one's life path.

That's when it hit her like a bolt of lightning—Annah married Jack on October 11th. She was convinced the universe was trying to tell her one of two things. Either its message is that it foresees a blissful marriage in her future; or it's a foreboding to run for the hills, to avoid another matrimonial disaster. Neither of these scenarios was remotely close to being on her immediate radar.

Annah plopped on the couch with an exaggerated huff. An emotional fire erupted deep within her, fueled by her jilted feelings and loneliness. It didn't take her long to realize it wasn't going to work out. She would call

Lance first thing in the morning to let him know how she felt.

But somewhere, during the course of a good night's sleep, Annah's heart softened and Lance had been absolved of all lapses in dating judgment, along with the realization that she wasn't quite ready to throw in the towel. She was certain he was worth a second chance, but made a promise to herself that if the next date didn't live up to her expectations, it was definitely over.

It was because of her unwillingness to give up that her second, third and subsequent dates were beyond all her romantic expectations. In fact, never in her wildest dreams could she have imagined a relationship to be so fulfilling. Often envying couples that seemed to have that perfect symmetry, she now understood the aching feeling of wanting to spend every moment together.

In a matter of months, they fell hopelessly in love. Lance became more than just a companion; he became her best friend, confidante and lover. Of course, as with any relationship, it had its trials and tribulations, but the good times definitely outweighed the bad. He was the glove that fit perfectly on her hand, her better half as they say—her soul mate.

They saw each other every day after work and would spend entire weekends together. Most times they did nothing more than grocery shop, share each other's chores, or watch a game, movie or favorite show on television. Every moment of every day was devoured by thoughts of Lance. He became her world and she became his.

Then there were the special moments, the ones that helped convince her that they were meant to be together. Like the time when he phoned her late in the evening when he saw on TV that there had been a prowler in her neighborhood. While she told him she was fine and not to worry, she loved his concern—his proof of real love. She feared, with unreasonable fear, of getting caught up in the idea of being in love, just for the sake of being in love; the idea of wanting it so much that it was manufactured instead of true. But in ways that only Lance could do, she was sure their love was tested and proven genuine.

Then there were the times, while she was away on business trips, he insisted on video chats every night before falling to sleep. They wanted to be certain that the last thing they saw before falling off was each other's faces. She loved that best. It was so, so loving. No ersatz romance created from some movie or book, but something real; and very appreciative.

Annah was grateful to have been given a second chance at figuring out the intricacies of a good relationship, but more importantly, to finally experience love—true love. She was thrilled that her life was moving forward in a positive direction, well in most aspects anyway, the caveat being the plaguing remnants of her divorce—the spite of her ex-husband.

Things went south when Jack found out Annah was dating. He said it was because he didn't want another man around his daughters. Annah, on the other hand, thought his motivation was to make her life miserable because he wasn't in it. Either way, Jack was bound and determined to chisel away at the utopian rock that made her feel loved and secure. Whatever his reason, she feared he would be successful in driving a wedge between she and Lance.

Annah felt that the only way to protect Lance from Jack's wrath was to exclude him from family functions where she knew Jack would be. But Lance didn't want her protection, he just wanted to be included and accepted at any cost. It was a hopeless feeling having to make a choice between happiness and control. For her daughters' sake, simply keeping the peace was paramount.

SPECTACULAR
CHRISTMAS

It was three weeks before Christmas and as a decade old tradition would dictate, Annah treated her family to the most anticipated event of the year, their annual trip to New York City. Annah loved the entire Yule season primarily for its significant meaning, but also because it sprinkles unequivocal magic into the air, generating an overall sense of happiness and good will.

Annah would begin planning the trip in early September by procuring the tickets to *Radio City Music Hall's Christmas Spectacular.* All other activities planned for the day revolved around the show time, so it was important to secure the date and time early on. She took full responsibility for the day's itinerary—from what they did to what time they did it. The train departure time kickstarted the day, so she made no qualms about having everyone standing on the boarding platform ten minutes before the train pulled into the station. It wasn't a matter of being in control, it was more so about getting the most out of their trip.

This particular year was very important to Annah because it was Lance's first trip to the City. She wanted him to experience the same magic she and her girls feel every time they go. The festivities would start at Macy's, taking pictures with Santa at Santa Land, which sets the tone for the rest of the day. Then they would embark on their twenty block trek to Radio City to marvel at the high-kicking, world renowned *Rockettes*. After the show, they would just grab a hot dog or pretzel from a street vendor and head down to St. Patrick's Cathedral. Annah felt this stop was important, to remind everyone what the season was truly about.

The next stop would be ice skating at Woolman's Rink in Central Park, which always proved to be a comical undertaking. To put it quite simply, this was the only time of year they would skate, so their butts were on the ice more than their blades.

Having worked up an appetite, dinner followed skating at a familiar haunt, Jekyll and Hyde's, which was only a block and a half from the Park. They loved this restaurant which always proved to be a unique and memorable time. The ghoulish staff, dressed for ghastly success, would interact with the guests at their tables usually with a diabolically themed, satiric act. It was the perfect opportunity to relax and reflect on the awesome things they had done that day.

Immediately after dinner, and on their way back to the train, they would stop to marvel at the magnificent, holiday tree that was grandly poised in Rockefeller Center. It towered to a height of nearly seventy feet, adorned with over thirty-thousand twinkling bulbs. No matter how tired they all felt, they made sure to capture this legendary tree and the heralding angels that stood before it, as a backdrop for their annual family portrait.

But, as meticulously as the day was planned, there was a small glitch. On this particular Saturday in December, the crowds were densely fierce, which ultimately translated to longer wait times and limited mobility—all factors that can't be predicted in advance. Flexibility became a necessary evil, so an on-the-fly adjustment to the itinerary needed to be made. The unfortunate compromise, they would have to skip ice skating if they were to leave the City at a decent hour.

Annah could tell that Lance became agitated by this abrupt change, which was out of character for him. He was typically a go-with-the-flow type of guy. She felt bad having made this last minute decision, but knew from experience it was in everyone's best interest. They still had to take pictures at the tree and endure the long haul back to the train.

She asks, "Is something wrong?"

"I'm just a little disappointed that we aren't going ice skating. If dinner doesn't take too long, will you reconsider?"

Trying to interpret his urgency, she explains, "It's been an extremely long day. We are all exhausted." She suggests, as a consolation, "We could come back in a few weeks to skate in Central Park, just you and I, ok?"

Before he had a chance to answer, the restaurant pager began to vibrate. "Well, that's us!" Annah announces. They check in with the maître d' and are seated on the top level, which was appropriately named, *The Attic*. Besides being famished and dehydrated, they agreed their biggest relief was to be off their sore and nearly blistering feet.

While everyone was ordering their drinks and appetizers, Lance leaned in to Annah asking if she would accompany him on a carriage ride through the Park. He knew how much she enjoyed it, having heard recounts from past years; and truth be told, she wanted to share that romantic experience with the love of her life. Besides, she thought it was the least she could do for having cancelled the skating last minute. They excused themselves from the table, leaving their entrée orders with the others, promising to be back before dinner was served.

Eagerly, they walk down to the Park. Annah watched as Lance became mesmerized by the dazzling pageantry of beautifully groomed stallions hitched to their respective carriages. The coachmen sat tall in their seats, aptly attired in long, black wool trench coats, white gloves and silk top hats.

Lance commented, "This is quite amazing! You don't see a sight like this every day."

They approach the first carriage in line, a white barouche. Their driver helped them up to their seats and offered them a woolen throw to keep them warm during the ride. Once he settled into his high seat up front, he signaled for his steed to begin its trot. With a slight tap from the reins, the beautiful white equine began to strut and the spindled wheels began to turn. Lance wrapped his arm around Annah hoping this would be the most romantic ride of her life.

The crisp winter night added to the uniquely defined ambience that only this grand city could offer. Their driver, who spoke with the most charming Irish brogue, was a Park trivia aficionado. As their horse clopped along the lamp lit streets, he gave a brief commentary on the history of certain landmarks that would otherwise have gone unnoticed by the average tourist. They passed the spot where they filmed the chess scene for the movie about *Bobby Fischer,* the American chess prodigy. Whether it was fact or fiction didn't matter, it was still a fascinating tidbit.

Lance suddenly became restless and fidgety. He removed his arm from Annah's shoulder and stared blankly at the empty seat across from them. Annah was concerned with his preoccupation, but didn't want to address his bizarre behavior until the ride was over. She just hoped he wasn't bored. She reached for his hand, but instead of clasping hers, he pulled the neatly tucked blanket from under his legs, stood, and replaced it on his vacant seat. Next thing she knew he was on the carriage floor. His baffling behavior prompted her to ask if he was feeling sick, or nauseous.

In a barely audible, crackled tone, he answers, "No, I'm fine!"

She followed up by asking if he had dropped something.

He softly mumbles, "No!"

The clip-clop of the horseshoes against the cobble-stones became very pronounced. So to fill the uncomfortable void, Annah began to mimic the rhythmic cadence, "clip-clop, clip-clop," hoping he would enthusiastically join in.

"What the hell is he doing down there?"

It dawned on her that maybe his contact lens popped out as a result of the dry and rushing air and he was groping the dark floor in hopes of finding it. She decides to offer her help, but he refuses and instead clenches her hand and stares intently into her eyes.

He clears his throat several times before reaching into the inner pocket of his pea coat. Without noticing what he had pulled out, Annah listens as Lance utters his first words in what seemed like forever, "Will you marry me?"

In a state of shock, Annah felt light-headed and stared at Lance in disbelief not realizing she hadn't acknowledged that he even asked a question.

He took a long breath and asked again, "Annah, will you marry me?"

She answered with the first thing that naturally came to her lips, "Yes, I will marry you!"

It took a few seconds for Annah to digest the moment and embrace the reality of what had just happened. They had looked at rings a couple of times and discussed the possibility, but this was so unexpected. She pulled Lance in close, expressing her overwhelming love for him, letting him know how moved she was by his ingenious planning of the perfectly romantic proposal. He innocently admits that he was going to do it on the ice at the skating rink, but this actually worked out much better.

They pulled up to the curb, at the end of the queue of carriages. Their driver turned to them offering his congratulations and if they would like him to take their picture. He climbed down from his perch, and Annah handed him her digital camera, posing with her newly decorated finger propped on Lance's chest. As cliché as this may sound, Annah wanted that moment to last forever.

On their walk back, Annah was thinking about how her daughters would react. They couldn't have seen it coming; hell, Annah didn't even see it coming. She was justifiably conflicted on how she would make her announcement. It wasn't until they were at the entrance of the restaurant that Annah decided it would be best to wait a day to break the news. Lance seemed disappointed, but said he understood and supported her decision.

It seemed like a good plan except for one relatively small detail. Someone was sure to notice her newly acquired piece of jewelry—namely a glittering engagement ring. Cleverly, she decides to keep her gloves on for the rest of the evening, suggesting her hands were still cold from the freezing temperatures outside. So, like a total imbecile, she wore her gloves through dinner and didn't take them off until she went to bed.

The next morning, when the house finally woke up, Annah called her daughters downstairs for a family powwow. She didn't want to drag this out, so as soon as they were all seated, she extended her hand allowing her news to announce itself. She gave them a moment for it to sink in before blurting out the obvious, "Lance proposed to me last night on the carriage ride and I accepted."

They stared at their mom, then the ring, then back at Mom. Her youngest thought it was amusing and started to giggle. She never was one to take any matter too seriously. The others sat motionless with their grinning mouths gaped open. Her oldest took the initiative to congratulate her and ask for a compilation of all the romantic details. All eyes were on Annah.

"Are you happy, Mom?" was the first of the barrage of questions.

"Yes, I am happy. I'm still in shock, but very happy!"

They all broke out in a contagious fit of giddy laughter, wanting to know the answers to all the typical questions like if Lance knelt down on one knee, or if Annah cried when he proposed. They crowded together on the floor, slinging one question after another, slumber party style like teenage girls talking about their latest crushes. They wanted all the particulars and Annah was more than willing to tell them whatever they wanted to know.

The one detail she wasn't ready to divulge was that the minute the ring was put on her finger, it wasn't only her hands that were cold—her feet suffered the same ailment. She wasn't sure if it was because she still had the bad taste of her first marriage lingering in her mouth, or if she wasn't sure she was ready to share her life with Lance till the end. Either way her concerns remained hidden and she convincingly displayed all the signs of being happily betrothed.

A WOLF IN SHEEP'S CLOTHING

A nnah had officially changed her relationship status to engaged, but that's about all that changed
when she accepted Lance's proposal. She wasn't wrap-
ping her mind around the entire concept of transitioning
to a shared life; she would conveniently shrink away from
the subject of her future nuptials. Honestly though, her
reservations weren't totally unfounded. She had already
taken a couple of swigs of that drink called 'freedom and
independence' and loved the way it tasted. She feared
that if she settled down, that delectable drink would no
longer be available; making it a commodity that would
become extinct over time.

So what was the next step? It was anyone's guess;
an arbitrary question to which there were no immediate
answers.

Months went by before either of them broached the subject of their future. It wasn't until early summer that Lance casually suggested combining resources, specifically selling both homes and purchasing a house together. Annah knew her children would be a little resistant to leaving the house they passionately called home. Quite honestly, Annah wasn't ready to give it up either. Her unyielding stance didn't fare well with Lance but, in her mind, if they were engaged and have pledged their love to each other, things would progress in time. If it's meant to be, it will be, regardless of temporary stumbling blocks.

Over time, those mounting blocks began to build a wall—a wall that was heightening between them. Annah began to compile a laundry list of dissimilarities, including their polar differences in parenting styles. Lance had a more laid back approach where Annah was more rigid and overly structured. She began to realize that maybe their children wouldn't blend as a unit; family functions and holidays would be a disaster, not to mention having all of them living under one roof. She was certain it would present ongoing challenges.

They began to argue more frequently, mostly about depthless, superficial issues. She attributes the growing animosity to her inflexible attitude—which was nothing more than a diversion to mask her fear of commitment. As a result, their relationship began to show signs of deterioration.

Annah was no longer on the pedestal Lance had placed her on. His whole demeanor changed. He was callous, secretive, and markedly aloof. Annah's defense mechanism forced her to adopt a 'whatever' attitude and she honestly didn't care if days went by where they didn't see each other. It had crossed her mind that his sudden disregard for her feelings was a pathetic attempt to make her grovel for the return of his undying affection, which she didn't succumb to.

In hindsight, however, she felt maybe she should have.

Lance began to glorify a particular woman at work who, ironically, he didn't care too much for just a few months prior, when things were good between him and Annah. All of a sudden, Denise was the greatest person in the world. Annah had only met her once, but as far as first impressions go, she perceived her as a snake in the grass; a person who couldn't be trusted. But Annah's opinion didn't matter. Lance had Denise walking on water.

When their relationship was inches away from hitting rock bottom, Annah felt she had nothing to lose by confronting Lance, hoping he would confess his true feelings for Denise. He assured Annah that he was still very much in love with her, and that he and Denise were 'just friends'. Annah begged to differ, especially when his actions were in direct conflict with his words.

The amount of time Lance and Annah spent together was reduced to once a week at best. After carefully considering all the dynamics that had come into play, Annah thought it was best, for them both, to call off the engagement. When she returned the ring to Lance, he didn't seem surprised or upset. He said he completely understood her decision. His reaction was a little dampening; she expected, or maybe wanted, a little more drama. After all, they had been engaged for a little over two years.

If he loved her so much, why didn't he put up more of a fight?

Had he secretly hoped for a break up so he could move on, or move in on Denise?

Annah admitted she still loved Lance and expressed an interest in casually dating, just nothing serious for a while. Lance, for whatever reason, interpreted it as a clean break, as in they were done altogether—forever. Honestly, Annah felt if the shoe were on the other foot, she may have reacted the same way. His ego was bruised and he probably figured if the engagement was called off, what kind of relationship could be built and nurtured in the future.

It wasn't until early April, a couple months after their 'disengagement' that Annah called Lance hoping sufficient time had passed and the breakup wounds had healed. It was a Saturday and Annah was on her weekly grocery run. She circled the parking lot a few times, landing a spot fairly close to the entrance. She sat for a moment staring at her phone; finally dialing Lance's number.

After three rings, he answers with a very frosty, distant, and confused, "Hello?"

She wasn't going to let his tone discourage her, so she rallied every ounce of cheerfulness from the depths of her being.

"Hi! I was just thinking about you and wondering how you've been."

"I'm just fine! I have to say, I didn't think I'd ever hear from you again."

Lance wasn't one to hold back or mince his words, but she wasn't prepared for such a chilly reception to her good intention.

The excruciating pause prompted Annah to fill the void with a story from her recent past.

"I had quite a scare last week."

She didn't wait for his acknowledgement; she just continued on, "I woke up one morning covered in blood. Sometime during the night I had a severe nosebleed. My face and neck were crackled with dried blood, and my pillowcase and bedding were saturated with darkened crimson stains. It was the weirdest thing!"

Annah waited for a sympathetic response, but he maintained his frigid stance.

"I'm not sure why you called, but I need more time."

Annah was confused by his needing more time. She wanted to ask what he meant by it, but wasn't sure she was ready for the answer. She simply suggests that he call when he's ready.

With no further comment, he closes with, "Ok, I have to get going...goodbye."

She was confounded by his arrogance and callousness. What the hell did he need more time for? That was the burning question. She was frustrated that he couldn't at least hold a civil conversation with her, but wasn't going to waste her mental energy over-analyzing the foundation for his hard-hearted attitude.

She refused to devote the rest of the weekend harboring anxiety, or second guessing her ill-timed decision to call Lance. She knew, eventually, the answer would present itself. And that it did. The universe, in all its complexity, delivered an answer to Annah's inbox first thing Monday morning. It was an email from Lance; but most definitely not the email she had hoped for.

"Hey. How are you doing? I wanted to tell you that I'm thinking about going on a date. I don't know 100% where we stand, but I think we said our good byes in our last email. I'm sure I'm not your biggest fan but I wanted to write and tell you. I hope to hear from you."

"Hope to hear from *me*?"

Lance had definitely gotten under her skin.

She contemptuously responds, without taking the time to think it through, "Have fun on your date!"

Then, adding insult to injury, she rashly supplements her scorn, "It's funny that you can write to tell me you are dating when I tried to talk to you, especially since you said you needed more time. Please don't write me anymore...I'm hurt. What you've done is unforgivable. Please—just leave me alone!"

What really got her blood boiling was the aforementioned 'last' email, where Lance had lovingly written, "I have no interest in anyone else, but I do have a desire to see you happy."

She was a jumbled mess of disoriented emotions. It had only taken him five short months to fall out of love, forget how special their relationship was and put himself back on the market. It was the fact that he had moved on so quickly that hurt her the most.

The tears streamed down her face. She had never experienced this type of pain; an emotional, gut wrenching, inconsolable pain whose cause was a plethora of deception, isolation and abandonment. Nothing made sense; her thoughts were hazy; she needed to leave work right away so she packed up and left. On her way home she called Lance, despite her explicit instruction for him to never talk to her again.

To her surprise, he answered.

Annah skipped the formalities and began her tirade, "Why after telling me that you needed more time, would you email me a few days later to let me know you were going on a date?"

She began to hyperventilate, but managed to ask, through her sniveling, "Who is the date with?"

He justifiably felt he shouldn't have to defend his actions or decisions to her or anyone else, so he smugly retaliates, "Does it matter who it's with?"

Unwilling to let him off the hook that easily, she insists, "Is it with Denise?"

His moment of hesitation spoke volumes. He knew the only way to appease Annah was to tell her what she wanted to hear.

"Yes, it is with Denise."

Annah's heart shattered. Even though she already knew the truth, his admission gave it validation. She couldn't breathe, speak, or retain a single thought; she was overcome by betrayal and despair. It was time that Annah took off her rose colored glasses where Lance was concerned and face the truth that she was once blinded by. In their final months together, Lance had a growing adoration for Denise.

Annah's appetite was hungering for more information, so she risks asking, "Do you love her?"

With no hesitation, he confides, "Yes, I do love her!"

Annah held the phone at a distance so he couldn't hear her insuppressible sobbing. All she could think about was his email from earlier in the day, informing her that he was *thinking* of going on a date. Now, almost eight hours later, he loves her? Something didn't quite add up.

Lance could tell Annah didn't have a handle on her emotions and asked if she was driving. She tells him she is, and that she's on her way home from work. He urges that she hang up and concentrate on the road before she gets into an accident, which Annah interpreted as he just wanted the call to end. There were no good-byes just an empty silence.

She doesn't recall what happened after that, but found herself standing on her patio, staring out into the woods that bordered the backyard. She leaned against the corner post in agonizing disbelief. Her thoughts were on how she was going to make amends, taking on the entire burden of blame, insisting that Lance had good reason to never want to see or speak to her again—which was the last thing Annah wanted. She felt she owed him an explanation or at least an apology for her estranged behavior. She dials his number after she regroups. To her amazement, he answers once again.

"Listen, Lance, I'm sorry I reacted the way I did. I had a feeling it was her and when you confirmed it, I was beside myself. So, I apologize for that."

There was silence.

Then finally, for the first time through all of this, the Lance she remembered emerged from his guarded shell and showed an ounce of genuine integrity.

"I didn't mean for this to happen the way it did. You should forget about me and move on with your life."

Annah paused for a moment before hanging up, knowing he was probably gone forever. She stared up to the heavens and somberly appealed, "Why is this happening to me?"

He was no longer the man she knew and loved. This woman, Denise, had totally moved in on him at work and used her cunning, conniving, obnoxious, overbearing kindness to win him over. She was like a wolf among a herd of sheep—lying low, waiting for the lonely single sheep to wander away so she could pounce on her vulnerable prey and claim it as her own.

Annah still couldn't bring herself to hate him. The reality was—she felt sorry for him. Denise had taken advantage of his good nature, his kindness, his innocence and gullibility. She gave him the attention he sought and treated him like a king. Who can blame him for falling victim to that?

The fact that he professed his love for Denise is what struck a chord with Annah. Less than five months prior he was proclaiming his love for her. How do you fall out of love, then back in love with someone else so quickly and easily?

Annah's familiar backyard landscape became indistinct, her home stood lifeless and eerily cold, her world became surreal. She was unable to bring anything into focus, and struggled to find answers, hope, and meaning in this lonely, desolate place that had captured and now held her prisoner.

"What the hell is happening to me?" she wondered.

Lance was hopelessly tattooed her mind, heart and soul, and she knew if she were to confide this in anyone, they would tell her to forget about Lance and get on with life. She didn't need to be told how to feel, or what to do. What she did need was a healthy dose of empathy.

Knowing her friends couldn't possibly understand, or tell her what she desperately wanted to hear, she sought the advice of on-line tarot card readings. Within the course of a day, she was up to five or more readings, at five dollars a pop. If she didn't like the spread of cards, she would pay for another reading. The only thing she wanted to hear was that Lance was thinking of her, that he realized he had made a huge mistake, and that the love they once shared would be renewed. She wasn't ready to give up hope.

So by the end of May, Annah resorted to desperate measures. She longed to hear his voice, and hoped if he heard hers it would stir some of those old feelings. She would offer only friendship, at least initially, with the ulterior motive to have him back in her life. How could he not agree to this gesture?

She dismissed every ounce of apprehension and summoned enough courage to compose an email asking him to meet up for drinks to *just talk*. Her email was somewhat elusive, but did not allude to anything more than drinks, talking, and a peace offering to remain friends. She wasn't prepared for his off-putting response; basically he let Annah know he couldn't and wouldn't do that to Denise.

"What the hell was I doing to Denise?" she thought.

She wasn't asking him to leave Denise or to cheat on her—it was just drinks and conversation. Not that she wanted him to, but he could have brought Denise. She resented his presumption of an underlying motive, despite the fact that he wasn't too far off the mark—Annah may have been hoping for and thinking about a reconciliation, but her intentions for meeting up were genuine. She couldn't wrap her mind around his juvenile behavior. It was inconceivable that this was the same person she was so in love with.

Annah had once read that no one has ever died from a broken heart. The reality is, you may not die in the conventional sense, but a part of you withers away. You become cold and detached, like a zombie walking through the motions of what used to be your life.

PLEAS FOR HELP

Annah came to appreciate all the singletons out there, especially when the weekend rolled around. Friday and Saturday nights definitively become the worst two nights of the week. When the clock struck five on Friday, ending the workweek, the socially active would cheerfully chant *TGIF*, while they exchanged detailed summations of their over-booked weekend plans, pausing only to complain they only had two days to fit it all in. Annah didn't dare spew off her pitiful weekend agenda, which would redundantly include house cleaning, laundry, bill paying, grocery shopping and if time allowed, lawn mowing.

She tried to maintain her sense of humor by poking fun at herself, "Yay, my weekend is complete! Who needs a social life anyway?"

She would spend her Friday nights going through unread emails and playing games on the computer, keeping the television on, mostly for company. She had become complacent about email management, so one particular night she decided to go through each one, one at a time; first responding to unanswered correspondence, then clearing out all advertisements. She came to one, however, that piqued her curiosity. It was an offer for a free psychic reading and felt the timing was impeccable.

Having felt it was no coincidence, more like an intervention undoubtedly sent by the universe, she carefully took the time to read it. It resonated with the discord in her life, cleverly depicting, almost verbatim, the struggles she was going through. Annah decided to send for the complimentary reading, which was based on a single question. She knew the one question had to be clear and concise to assure an accurate response. After several minutes of writing down different versions of the same query, she finally decided on, "Will my ex-lover ever come back?" She completed all the required information, proofed it for errors, and clicked the icon to submit her question.

Annah spent the next few hours second guessing her choice of words. Maybe it was too ambiguous. She pounded her forehead with the palm of her hand thinking, "How will the psychic know I was referring to Lance and not my ex, Jack?"

"What an idiot! I had one chance, and I blew it!"

Haste makes waste was a fair assessment of her impulsiveness. At that point, it was a done deal and all she could do was wait to see how her question was interpreted, and what the reading revealed based on that interpretation. The offer didn't mention a turnaround time, but she assumed it would be within the next few days.

"What the heck!" she thought. "It was free and will probably be an interesting read, at the very least." Her optimistic side held on to the belief that it would reveal the answer she desperately longed for; or more so, wanted to hear.

After a grueling five days of anxious anticipation, she sees the free reading sitting in her inbox just waiting to be opened, along with a dozen or so less significant items. So like a child on Christmas morning, she opened all the little, more non-essential items first so she could focus on the pièce de résistance. Now with all other emails cleared out, she could focus her attention on what the psychic predicted for her future.

She swirled the mouse around a couple of times, preparing herself for this revelation. Then, with a single click, she opens it. There it was, right in front of her— the moment of truth. She didn't bother reading through the niceties preceding the link for the attachment; she went right for the kill. The attachment was a page and a half and only briefly addressed her question. It covered all areas like lucky days, health forecast, immediate future and the ever so important, lucky numbers. It danced around the answer to her question like a young child avoiding an imminent scolding, but was just enough to bait her into wanting a more detailed report, which was available for a fee. She willfully swallowed the lure, hook, line and sinker.

Annah felt depreciated and ashamed that her life had turned to psychic readings and hopeless dreams; and also felt guilty for this self-indulgence because it was such a frivolous amenity, considering her funds were rapidly diminishing. Only time would tell if the investment would pay off and give her the answers she sought; bringing back the joy and happiness that had been stripped from her life.

So after ten days of waiting, and still no report, Annah was beginning to think she had become the latest victim of one of those internet scams that prey on impulsive, unsuspecting fools like her. How could she have been so gullible? But being a true believer that we all learn from our mistakes, she chalked it up to her lack of diligence; a costly lesson learned.

It was June 18th, Father's Day, and Annah's daughters were celebrating the day with their dad. She didn't relish the thought of being alone with her memories, or thoughts of what could have been that sporadically crash in to her feeble mind like a hurricane coming to shore; relentless and damaging.

She realized that reaching out to someone would help get her through this difficult time, but it wasn't as if she could just pick up the phone and burden someone with her tales of woe—not on Father's Day. But an over-powering wave of anxiety was building inside of her, causing an urgent need to reach out to somebody—anybody.

About a year ago, Annah attended a psychic reading party arranged by a close friend. One by one, they were called to a back room where they received a personalized tarot card reading. Annah went in with an open mind and immediately the astrologer, Isabelle, remarked in a firm, yet gentle tone, "You are a force to be reckoned with!"

Unsure of what she meant, Annah jokingly replied, "I sure am!"

Isabelle, probably about sixty years old with a fragile, somewhat petite frame, bared the resemblance of a haggard crone, not in a hideous sense, but more along the lines of time worn with a mystical, enchanting air. She gestured for Annah to sit in the folding chair facing her on the opposite side of the table.

Without making eye contact, Isabelle asked Annah if there was anything specific she wanted to ask for her reading. She didn't, at the time, so Isabelle assiduously placed the cards in a cross-type configuration and proceeded with a generic reading. She gazed intently at the spread of cards before she began her interpretation of what the cards envisaged for Annah's future.

At one point, Isabelle looked stumped as she placed her forefinger on one particular card. "I see that you are content with your life and have a wonderful family, however, it is showing an involvement with a married man. He is pursuing you and is deceptive in his intentions. Steer clear of this one; he will never leave his wife."

Annah immediately reflected on a guy at work that she felt was becoming a little too comfortable around her. He confided that his marriage was on the rocks and dropped several hints alluding to a serious relationship between them if his marriage were to end. Annah was flattered by his proclamation, but knew, in the long run, it wouldn't be conducive to a healthy working relationship, so she let him down easy.

Overall, Annah was impressed with Isabelle's reading and knew if she were to get the answers she needed regarding her current, waning sense of reality, she needed to get in touch with her. She did an online search for psychics in the area, but there were no listings that referenced the name Isabelle. Annah remembered being given an audio recording of their session. She frantically rummaged through her junk drawer where she found the cassette and printed on its case was the name and phone number of the psychic extraordinaire.

She stared at the number for a few moments wondering if she was doing the right thing by inviting possible truths she wasn't prepared to hear. But if anyone could help her through this nonsensical nightmare, it would be Isabelle. Annah grabbed a piece of paper and pen, and sat at the kitchen table waiting to hear that gentle and comforting voice that would soon settle her racing mind, and soothe her aching heart.

"Hello, Isabelle speaking!"

"Hi! You probably won't remember me, but I had a reading done by you at a friend's house several months ago and…." Annah was anxious to complete her sentence but was abruptly cut off.

"I do remember you. Your voice is very distinct to me. I can also feel your energy and sense that something is causing an upheaval in your life. I have a couple of things to finish up and then I will prepare your cards.

Can you call back later today, around 6:00 tonight, when I can give you a proper reading?"

"Yes. I will call back then. Thank you so much!"

It was only four in the afternoon, so Annah had two hours to monitor the clock, wishing she had some sort of mental telepathic capabilities that could fast forward to six o'clock. She found it virtually impossible to contain her nervous energy or engage herself in an activity that would help her pass the time. Her heart began to pound and tears flowed down her cheeks.

Not again! I can't do this again. Eventually I'll have no tears left, then what?

Annah went over to the sofa, deciding maybe a nap would make it all go away or at least anesthetize the pain. It didn't take long for her to fall asleep, but sat up after an hour in a panic, confused and disoriented; she felt she had overslept and missed the call. To her relief, she hadn't and the catnap helped in reviving her spirits. She felt more in control of her thoughts and emotions.

It was five minutes till call time and Annah finished up the questions she had prepared for the one hour reading. She dials Isabelle's number. A man answers and tells Annah to hold on while he gets his mother. In the interim, Annah feels solacing warmth and a general feeling of hopefulness.

"What is it that is bothering you, dear?"

Annah felt inclined to answer, but Isabelle continues, "I sense something is terribly wrong or unsettled in your life. I have spread your cards and I see you have experienced some sort of loss; this loss is causing you tremendous grief."

"I...I...I...." Annah stammers, searching for the right words.

"Take a few deep, cleansing breaths and let me know when you are ready to continue."

Annah regains her composure.

"Isabelle, I feel like I'm experiencing a mental break-down. I can't put anything in perspective and nothing in my life makes sense. I need answers concerning a man whom I loved deeply. We are no longer together, but I miss him so much. I need for you to tell me that he feels the same; that he loves me; realizes his mistake; and will soon be back in my life."

There was a moment of silence.

"Isabelle?"

"Are you still there?"

"What do you see?"

"What are the cards telling you?"

"Please say something!"

And that she does.

"He doesn't love you anymore; he's with another. You need to let go and move on. I see you will have a happy future, but I don't see this man in your life."

Annah pleaded that Isabelle was mistaken and misin-terpreted the meaning of the spread.

"Had I mentioned that the love Lance and I shared was that special kind of eternal love?"

"Are the cards showing you that?"

In a calm but firm tone, Isabelle confirmed her initial analysis that the relationship was over and the importance, for Annah's mental health, to move on with her life. Annah couldn't speak and her breathing was labored, to the point of hyperventilating. Isabelle appeared annoyed that Annah wasn't accepting what the tarot reading had unquestionably determined, so she offered to light a candle in hopes of attracting angels to keep a careful watch over her; to protect and guide her through this crisis.

Isabelle whispers with heartfelt compassion, "I will also pray for you."

Annah listened intently, hoping to hear Isabelle recant her first interpretation of the cards, replacing the gloomy forecast with a sunnier forecast that she and Lance would be reunited very soon. But, in her delusional frenzy, Annah hadn't realized Isabelle had already hung up. Just like that, Isabelle had abandoned her just like Lance did.

Why can't these people see I'm pleading for help?

Instead of closing the door in my face, they should be more concerned with my mental stability.

Damn it! I'm being dragged into the depths of darkness and no one seems to care....

Annah knew Lance had completely obliterated her from his life and any lingering remnants of what they shared were probably destroyed by now or long forgotten. He had obviously lost all feeling and love for her and is now comfortably settled in his new life. She envied his forward direction and couldn't seem to get a handle on where her life was headed. She was at a standstill. The more she thought about how they had drifted so far apart, the more distraught she became.

She was turning into a skeleton of a person, far from the person she once enjoyed being. She had shattered hopes, empty dreams and a very bleak outlook on life. Beyond a shadow of a doubt, she was experiencing a severe bout of depression; a total breakdown. The advertisements she had often seen about depression were true, you lose interest in everything you once enjoyed.

Annah had to make conscientious attempts to rally her energy and get through the day as effortlessly as possible. She didn't want anyone to know she was *losing it*, so she concealed her underlying emotional upheaval by acting as normal as possible—at least in public.

LETTING GO &
MOVING ON

In order to start the process of letting go, Annah knew she needed to stop coddling the notion that only Lance could make her feel loved, secure, and happy; that he was the only one that could make her feel whole again. She also knew it meant severing all emotional ties and flushing them forever in her mental toilet. You see, it's not that she didn't want to let go and move on, it was more so that she was in a holding pattern where her emotions were in control.

Annah heard her daughters fumbling with their keys at the front door and knew she had to pull herself down from the cloud of darkness that had consumed her for most of the day. She didn't want them to know what she was going through or what was happening to her. Being the matriarch of the family, she had to remain strong and not let them feel she could be weakened so easily.

Her daughters had a great day with their dad, grandparents and cousins, and their jubilance pulled Annah out of her black hole, at least for the time being. They were excited to share their updates on what was going on in the lives of her ex-relatives. Aunt Jo was sporting a mustache as a result of her menopausal condition; Uncle David, who had just turned fifty, had an affair with a twenty-five year old and the two are expecting little David next month; and dear Cousin Adrienne finally come out of the closet and brought her partner along to meet the family. Annah used to love hearing the juicy tidbits of gossip from family functions, but not on that particular day; she was struggling to stay focused.

She gave everyone hugs and kisses and went up to bed. But as tired as she felt, her mind was churning up the residual effects of the heartache she suffered earlier. She tossed and turned for hours, and finally ended up going downstairs for a drink and to work on a few crossword puzzles, hoping it would make her tired. The house was quiet, her girls had since gone to bed and now she was wide awake. The last thing Annah needed was quiet time alone. The louder the silence, the noisier Annah's mind became. Eventually her mind and body collapsed. She had finally fallen asleep.

The next day, Annah woke up rested and brimming with industrious enthusiasm. She had determined that her only chance to return to normalcy was to move on, and the first step was to alter her mindset. She knew it was going to be no easy feat, and the road would be bumpy, but expected it to be worth the effort. It was time to listen to truths that Lance was gone forever, no matter how painful they were to hear, time to climb out of the mire of denial and high time she regained her status as an ambitious, courageous and successful woman.

Her new regimen was to begin by doing the unthinkable; a strategy Annah swore was against her core principles—signing up with a reputable, online dating service. It took her over an hour to fill out page after page of redundant personal information that felt more like a standardized test than a dating profile. Suffice it to say, this chemistry driven, psychologically proven dating site now knew more about Annah than she knew about herself.

After her exhaustive completion of the survey, she wondered why so many singles put themselves through such a rigorous process to find a compatible mate? Humorously remarking, "What does my favorite childhood toy, shampoo brand or the name of my first pet have to do with compatibility?"

She only signed up for the introductory offer, a three month subscription, which she regretted the moment she entered her credit card information and accepted the terms of the agreement. She feared she had just become the perfect match for a sexual predator.

With her first task behind her, she was ready to get on with her day of non-stop productivity. The stereo went on, slightly louder than usual; the first load of laundry began to agitate in the washer; the computer was powered down; and the feather duster was propped in her hand, but not for cleaning. She was using it as a pseudo microphone, singing along with her favorite songs like a diva at a rock concert.

Feeling motivated and highly energized, she even broke out in a free-style dance that she choreographed as she went along. Her kids, had they been awake, probably would have expressed their honest opinion on Mom's out-dated dance moves. But, because no one was around, she didn't care how ridiculous she looked kicking it old-school.

She was cheerfully singing along with a popular oldie, but stopped once she realized it was one of her and Lance's favorite songs. In fact, the next song, and the song after that were also on a play list she and Lance created, all reminders of the past. She felt it was a cruel attempt to rattle her already unsteady emotions. It caused shivering chills to travel down her spine.

She was convinced the universe was playing tricks on her. It knew her mind was one cent short of a dollar, and with the slightest provocation she would be swallowed up by a relentless, thirsty pool of quicksand. The one thing she didn't want, or need, was to be reminded of the things she was trying so hard to forget. That being said, she turned off the music and finished up her chores in total silence.

As the days passed, Annah was just going through the motions of her normal, everyday routines. In short, she had gone on auto-pilot—shower, work, eat, sleep, then repeat. Her bedtime was getting earlier and earlier every day; she didn't want free time to think about what went wrong in her life. Oftentimes, during the day, she would get mental images of Denise and Lance together, making memories that should have been hers. The very thought of him being intimate with someone else was more pain than she could bear. She continued to struggle with not knowing what she had done in life that was so terrible that she deserved this.

In a final attempt to find an antidote to this life-altering quandary, she searched for articles on how to find closure when a relationship ends, such as this one had. There had to be others out there that had similar experiences. She stumbled across a few interesting pieces that were no doubt written solely for the comedic value. For instance, one suggestion was to disjoin his family jewels and proudly display them in the curio cabinet as conversation pieces. She admits the mental image alone sparked a giggle or two.

On a more humane note, it was suggested to collect all tokens from the relationship, such as trinkets, letters, cards, etc. that were collective reminders, toss them into a roaring fire and mass destroy them once and for all. Some even said it helped to eulogize the mementos while the crackling inferno reduced them to ash. The premise being, if you destroy those outmoded, emotionally consuming pieces of history, you will find the closure you were otherwise denied.

Annah went through all her drawers, closets, and stored boxes collecting anything that remotely resembled a souvenir from the relationship and piled them on my kitchen table. She wanted to sort through them first to make sure she didn't discard anything of value—monetary value, or so she said. First item up for incineration was a photo taken at Santa Land from last Christmas. But when she took one look at the picture, all the memories from that day came rushing back. She couldn't get rid of it, it meant too much to her and besides, what if they were to reunite one day? She would have no physical recollection of the fun and loving times they shared together.

I know, I know—that was the whole point!

Now that she was back at square one, she wished she had a confidante that understood how hard this was for her. Her closest friends were charitable in extending their unsolicited opinions, but in the grand scheme of things, it provided little to no comfort. All she wanted to hear was how her feelings were healthy and that she would heal from this someday.

What she didn't appreciate hearing, but appeared to be the general consensus, were things that alluded to the fact that she was too good for him and he was just a loser anyway. Honestly, she didn't want to *do better*; she felt he was the best for her. It was hard for her to understand why her friends weren't confirming that her feelings were real and natural, and assuring her that there was a shining light at the end of that proverbial tunnel.

Annah began to rely on the sage advice of her daily horoscopes as her source of guidance and direction. It was uncanny, but the forecasts were attuned to her current situation; as if they were written specifically for Annah. She became obsessed, and this preoccupation had become an essential component in her life.

The daily readings had her hungering for more, so to satisfy this appetite, she went on to read the weekly, monthly and annual predictions as soon as they were available. She yearned for clarity, to know how her life was going to unfold as far in advance as possible.

As the days passed, between the online tarot readings and daily horoscopes, there was no doubt in her mind that messages were being sent from some higher power. No matter when she consulted with these psychic sources, the assessment of the state of her life was precise. Not only was it on the mark, she was given guidance on navigating the tricky waters along the path of her personal journey; warning her of possible pitfalls and inherent dangers.

She found the forecast for the month of June quite captivating, "This month you will receive an offer. It is something you would normally dismiss as inconsequential, but it is advisable that you not pass this up. It will be life-changing."

A calming euphoric energy briefly dissolved her tensions. She knew, in her heart, it could only mean one thing—she would be receiving a communication from Lance, welcoming her back into his life with open arms. She was ecstatic—life was good!

Her only reservation—what if she was dreadfully wrong?

She would check her email as soon as she got to work. If there were no emails from Lance, she didn't become unraveled—she knew she had the entire month of June to realize this prophecy.

THE BREAKDOWN

About seven years back, after Annah's youngest daughter was officially in school full time, she decided to rejoin the workforce. She had done administrative work in the past, but was yearning for something more challenging, mentally stimulating; something she would enjoy doing for the rest of her work career. After extensive research and on-line career evaluations, she decided to study software engineering.

She found a reputable school in the area and enrolled for the upcoming session. It was a rigorous course, but she excelled and liked it a lot. A few months after graduation, she became a nine-to-fiver once again as a computer programmer. She was confident, enthusiastic, and absolutely thrilled as she embarked on this new chapter of her life. Her only concern was that programming, inherently, is mentally challenging and requires a high degree of focus and concentration.

She left that company after five years of service, opting for a company closer to home. Her primary duties there were to write and maintain software programs, along with being last on the help desk call queue. She loved her job, at least in the beginning. But as the months went by her responsibilities increased, including a higher demand for client specific programs. This meant more complex and intricate coding details. As a result, Annah started to come in to work earlier, along with skipping lunches and working from home just to keep up with her assigned workload.

The combination of having to answer help desk calls, programming more sophisticated programs and meeting the expectations of her micromanaging supervisor, only served to amplify the anxiety that was already at an all-time high because of her personal struggles. It came to a point where several times throughout the work day she had to walk away from her desk to regroup.

In her already frenzied and fragile condition, she was becoming more sensitive to the bustling and increased noise levels in her immediate work area. It was challenging enough to effectively do her job in a low volume atmosphere, imagine twenty or so people all talking at once—some even shouting across the room.

It progressively became intolerable. She presented her concerns to her unscrupulous supervisor, who was adept at exhibiting an outward display of compassion and care. But privately, Annah knew better. He promised to look into something to shield or block the noise. But, being a self-centered, arrogant jerk, he never did anything about it. Quite frankly, Annah believed he ignored her request because it didn't benefit his upward climb to supreme power, an executive position he'd had in his sights for a while.

The unfortunate reality was, it wasn't going to happen and Annah knew it. The department manager, who was no better, didn't even know Annah existed. Heck, he couldn't even get her name right. One day, while on a conference call with a prospective client, he was going through the introductions and drew a blank when he came to Annah. As if pulling a name out of a hat, he introduces her as Sophia. She didn't react or correct him, but thought *what an idiot!* She wasn't sure if it was in jest, but since that day when he passed her desk, he would refer to her as Sophia. Being a trooper, from that day forward she learned to go-with-the-flow and answer to her new name.

Annah waited weeks for her noise reduction request to get approved, if it had even been acknowledged in the first place, but guessed after months of waiting, it wasn't in the cards. Work had become unbearably demanding; her workload was overwhelming; programming requests were coming in at record speed; neither her supervisor nor her team knew the complexity of her job; the noise levels were unforgivable; the walls were closing in and her mind was swirling like a cyclone, picking up her thoughts on its destructive path of reckless devastation and randomly strewing them in all directions.

The music that was piped in through the company-wide speakers, which had always played upbeat generic tunes, now contained satanic messages that she was convinced were playing just for her—the devil was trying to get in her head. She desperately wanted to cover her ears and scream for it to stop, but feared looking ridiculous—no one else seemed fazed by these diabolical lyrics.

She was trying hard to concentrate, but was reeling out of control. She couldn't cope any longer; something was terribly wrong. Not daring to share this lapse in her mental faculties with anyone, she kept it to herself. The last thing she needed was to be ostracized or ridiculed for her sudden abnormality.

That's when her mind snapped—she was literally going crazy.

THE GIFT

It was July 1st and Annah had an appointment with her optometrist, a routine visit for a vision check to renew her contact prescription. She was just about to leave the house when she was overcome by an acute panic attack. The very thought of having to sit in a waiting room with total strangers had her petrified, virtually to the point of canceling the appointment.

She feared she would innocently initiate a conversation about the weather that would metastasize into a discussion about the demoniacal ideations that were destructively impregnating her mind. Her sensibilities assured her she would refrain from such inappropriate chatter, but wasn't completely confident of an involuntary takeover.

There were five or so patients who had arrived before her so she deliberately sat as far away from them as possible. Restlessly perched on the edge of her chair, she tried to preoccupy herself by holding a conversation with herself, internally of course. The two proponents of this conflicting dialogue were pro and con. Con argued that if she didn't leave immediately, the unthinkable could happen and she would be ostracized for sure; while pro, being the more rational personality, persuaded that once she got through this appointment, she would have her prescription and be in the comfort of her home in no time. Needless to say, she erred on the side of rational and rode out the storm.

Feeling assured with her decision, she settled into her seat wondering how she was going to fill her wait time. She humorously broke down the protocols of waiting room etiquette. First, you try your damnedest to avoid eye contact, because once it's established, you can write off the next fifteen minutes in a superficial exchange of meaningless jabber; second, you make your first round of observations, admiring the wall art and other décor that serve no other purpose than to break the boredom with visual stimulation; third, you play the guessing game of who will be called in next and the order thereafter; and lastly, you rifle through the stack of outdated reading material, eventually picking up the magazine on top of the pile, which ultimately diverts your attention away from blankly staring at the clock on the wall.

Annah's reading choice was a magazine on dimensional and illusion art forms. She hoped it was enough to distract her for the next twenty minutes or so. Having just opened the cover, she overheard someone whisper, "This is taking forever!" She canvassed the small room to see whose voice it could have been, but everyone seemed to be preoccupied with something or another.

"I must be hearing things!" she contends.

Then, she heard it again.

"What is going on?"

In the absence of any other explanation, she concluded she was able to read people's thoughts. The non-verbal communications increased in intensity and volume.

An impatient businessman complained, "I have a meeting in an hour—this is ridiculous."

A frazzled mother, proclaims, "If I don't get called next, I'm leaving. It's almost nap time and Nicholas is already driving me crazy."

"It can't be!" Annah thinks, her senses reeling.

"This is absurd! I can read minds?"

She knew she sounded borderline psychopathic, but it was really happening and quite frankly, she found it amusing.

As the room emptied, the voices were gradually replaced by the soft classical music that had been playing in the background. It was as if everything had returned to normal, as if it never happened at all. Maybe she had just drifted off and dreamed the whole thing up. She laughed to herself and went back to admiring the beautiful reproductions of artwork in the magazine that was still resting in her lap.

Shuffling through the pages of the distinctive works of art, she paused at a section entitled, *3D Art Gallery*. The introductory paragraph provided instructions on how to view and decipher the depth perceptional images.

Basically, without focusing on any one part of the image, a shape will magically pop out of the original muted image. She gave the first one a try. After only a few seconds, she saw a star pop out of the picture.

She continued on, picture after picture and each time, after a split second gaze, she knew exactly what the obscured image was. Between the earlier voices and now the deciphering of hidden images, it was clear to Annah, she was developing some sort of extra-sensory power—a gift if you will.

Annah gathered her personal belongings and set them on her lap. She didn't want to leave anything behind in the chair when she got called, which she knew would be soon. In the few minutes before she went in, she had an epiphany that her optometrist was going to tell her that her vision had actually improved since her last visit. Mind you, her vision had been deteriorating since she was in elementary school.

"The doctor will see you know!"

Annah was escorted to the examination room, where the doctor immediately began the normal tests. He rolled his stool over to the desk where he recorded the updated data on her chart. After a deep breath, he scooted back to the examination chair where Annah had been sitting. Slowly taking off his glasses, he slips the temple into the side of his mouth and reports, "You are not going to believe this—your vision has improved." Sensing explicit bewilderment, she knew he was perplexed. Annah, on the other hand, felt a stronger connection with the gift she was developing.

He smiled and asked if she had any other questions or concerns. Annah did have one concern. The week before the appointment, one of her daughters noticed a peculiar discoloration in both her eyes. She best described it as a halo-like arc on the outer rim of the upper part of her iris. Her optometrist had seen a full ring around the iris, which was typically the result of cholesterol deposits, but admitted he had never seen a partial arc like the one Annah had. He was certain it was nothing to worry about, but would note it on her chart. Annah took his word for it; anyway, it was hardly noticeable unless it was pointed out.

When Annah got home, she went on the internet to find out more about cholesterol deposits. She did an image search to see what it commonly looked like. In the images displayed, the iris was completely encircled by a white ring. Not one picture showed just an arc or halo. She would keep an eye on this (no pun intended) to see if the arc remained the same, or if it gradually formed a ring.

Annah walked around for the next few weeks experimenting with her new gift, which made her feel incredibly powerful. It could have all been in her mind, but she was able to sense things before they happened and knew what people were thinking before they said anything. She felt herself changing but hadn't yet decided if that was good or bad.

It was Monday, July 10th and Annah had just gotten back from her lunch break. She felt extremely nauseous, faint and dizzy. Her first thoughts were that either her lunch didn't agree with her or the exposure to the blistering heat had gotten the better of her. The dog days of summer were in full force; it was the fifth day of a heat wave that had temperatures peaking in the high nineties with dangerously high humidity levels. It wouldn't have been surprising if her sudden ill feeling was a result of dehydration, or the fact that she had transitioned from the air-conditioning in the office to the oppressive heat outside and vice versa.

She took two ibuprofen, drank an entire bottle of water, but the symptoms did not subside. She began to sweat profusely and her skin became cold and clammy. When she attempted to stand up to go to the ladies' room, her legs buckled and went limp; she plopped back into her chair to avoid a total collapse. The room began to spin around her, gradually picking up speed; she felt like she was in the eye of a storm.

She struggled to suppress the urge to scream at the top of her lungs, "What's going on?"

But instead of making a total fool of herself, she stealthily made her way to the emergency stairwell just a few yards away. There she sat, with her head in her hands as tears streamed down her face. She was losing all sense of reality and knew it was vital that she leave work immediately; she needed to sort out what was happening and avoid embarrassing herself in the presence of her co-workers.

At a little after one-thirty, she composed and sent an email to her supervisor requesting vacation time for the rest of the day, and the next day, simply explaining she felt ill. Avoiding contact with her co-workers, she quickly cleared her desk, shut down her computer, grabbed her things, and left. As she pulled out of the parking lot, she realized the potential of what may have happened had she stayed. Her mental acuities had taken a huge hit, but she managed to pull herself together long enough to make it home safely.

When she pulled up to her house, it was a great relief to see the driveway empty. She needed to embrace the quiet time, sort everything out, try to make sense of how she was feeling; and what caused the erratic episode at work. She poured herself a glass of wine and nestled into her comfy, over-sized living room chair.

Now that she was able to relax, she felt it was safe to rewind to the events earlier in the day. What had caused her disorientation? Why did her mind career out of control? It didn't take her long to realize that going back in time, to rehash the confusion, wasn't such a great idea after all. Her thoughts began to scatter once again, like a twister in her head, picking up fragments of thought and strewing them everywhere.

She began to plead relentlessly to the barrenness that surrounded her, "What the hell is happening to me?"

Unfortunately, for the countless questions she had, the answers were not forthcoming, at least not any time soon. Annah decided resting may settle her mind and hopefully slow her thoughts down to a manageable level. She went upstairs to her bedroom and burrowed comfortably in her bed. Without much effort, she felt her body begin to dispel the pressure and tension that had escalated throughout the day and off to sleep she went.

When Annah finally awoke several hours later, the house was dark. While she was sleeping, her daughters had come home and already gone to bed. Still a bit groggy, she stumbled out of bed and trudged downstairs to make some soothing, chamomile tea and watch a show, hopefully a comedy.

She fell asleep on the couch around midnight while, ironically, battling to stay awake. She had purposely kept the television on for background noise; she didn't like the feeling of being alone. Around three in the morning, she was awakened by programmed music that plays when the network goes off-air. The song that was playing, she later found out, was "Crazy" by Gnarls Barkley. The lyrics, though audible, were drawled and bellowed in a loathsome tone; hauntingly reminiscent of a demonically inspired incantation where he recounts a time when he loses his mind; intimately detailing the deep emotionality it evokes and steady decay of control. He concludes, as if personally counseling, "Well I think you're crazy—just like me."

Annah was scared. She knew, deep in her soul, someone or something was with her. Frightened and alone, she had nowhere to go and no one to talk to. It was the first time she had heard this song that eerily resonated with her state of mind.

She had entered a dark, desolate place. Her world had become very still. It was as if all animate objects became frozen in time and the sound of silence became frightfully deafening.

"Maybe I'm dreaming."

But if she were dreaming, how come, no matter how hard she tried, she couldn't wake herself up? Because this was no dream—it was very, very real!

That was the catalyst that woke her up to the realization that something very bizarre was happening to her.

She had convinced herself that this message was sent to her from some other-worldly place and its intent was to either frighten her or let her know of an impending condition that was about to consume her life. She was definitely rattled and unmistakably frightened.

Annah stayed awake reading magazines and doing crossword puzzles to make sure she was up to call her doctor at eight o'clock sharp. She wasn't going to return to work until she knew what was wrong with her, and more importantly, what caused her episode. Fortunately she was able to make a mid-morning appointment.

"Good Morning, Annah!" Dr. Oliver was always so pleasant with his soft-spoken voice and caring smile. Just his presence put Annah at ease.

"Good morning, Doctor!"

"So, what brings you here this morning?"

Annah didn't know where to start or even how to explain what was happening without sounding like a total lunatic.

Dr. Oliver had been Annah's doctor for the past few years, ever since her former family doctor retired. At that time, her entire medical file had been transferred to his office, which didn't include any family history of mental illness. Up until this visit, Annah had only been treated for minor ailments like strep, sinus infections and the flu; otherwise her annual exams were normal.

"I feel I've reached a pinnacle of despair and can't seem to pull myself together. I left work early yesterday after having a meltdown. I feel sad, lonely, confused, tired, and totally lack motivation."

Dr. Oliver noted everything Annah said and together they went through all of Annah's symptoms, which also included feeling worthless, hopeless, withdrawal from things she enjoyed and from life in general.

He sat back in his high-back, executive leather chair, cleared his throat, raised his chin and asked, "Has something significant happened in your life—something life changing, or some sort of loss that you feel has disrupted your life?"

"I had a bad breakup that I can't seem to get over, along with the fact that work has become extremely demanding."

"Also, and I think more importantly, I recently had an experience I can only describe as bizarre. I was at a neighbor's gathering. Everyone was talking, all around me."

Dr. Oliver raised one brow a bit.

"I felt like I was dreaming and watching and hearing them talk, and they acted like I wasn't there. I don't think they were intentionally being rude, they just never seemed to notice I was there."

"That's part of depression, an overwhelming sense of paranoia that triggers irrational thoughts and feelings."

He diagnosed Annah with anxiety and depression, which brought her relief to have her illness identified, but conflicted on what it all meant for her immediate future. Annah didn't know anyone who had been diagnosed with this type of illness, so she was entering a new and unfamiliar arena.

Annah took the rest of the week off from work, which was strongly recommended by Dr. Oliver, who felt she needed time to rest and recuperate. She would see him in a week for a follow-up and, if necessary, further treatment. Annah realized she owed her supervisor an explanation for her abrupt departure the day before, and for having to take the next few days off. She composed and sent an email offering the best explanation she could summon, given the unique circumstance.

I felt the need to explain my current situation with you. The reason I have been so out of it lately is because I've been suffering from anxiety and depression. I went to the doctor and was basically told that my life had to slow down a little. It's not just work, but my personal life as well. I have a doctor's note to stay home the rest of the week to recuperate and relax. I do value my job, but at the rate I was going I wasn't benefiting anyone. This has been a harsh reality for me to face, let alone to share with anyone. I don't know how you want to handle this, but I do need this time. I know I have pending work obligations and I fully intend to complete them, from home. Please let me know your thoughts.

Annah was bothered by his response. He asked her to send an email to her work team, letting *them* know she wouldn't be in. She felt awkward enough opening up to him, there was no way she was going to give personal information to her peers. She wondered if he had even read the entire email and, if he had, how could he have been so insensitive.

Feeling she had no other choice, she reluctantly wrote and sent the email. She left out the details about her illness, for obvious reasons, and merely explained that she had personal matters to attend to and wouldn't be in until the following week.

Several days had passed since the 'episode'. She hadn't eaten anything, but had no appetite. All she did was lie on the sofa all day; the mere thought of getting up wore her out. She had no drive and a depleting supply of energy.

Every day she waited for a miracle to waltz into her life and restore the happiness that was taken from her without so much as a warning. She faithfully checked her email several times a day in case Lance had a change of heart and tried to contact her, knowing, or shall we say hoping, it was only a matter of time before he realized he'd made a mistake and wanted her back. She was certain of it.

Every time she thought about work, her head began to throb. She was beginning to fear the worst. Would she ever be able to program again? Was her employer upset that she had taken time off? Are they going to fire her as a result? She struggled with all these questions, especially because she had no answers. She couldn't think straight; her thoughts were all over the place. For her sanity's sake, she needed to work on getting better before attempting to put her life back in order.

THE CONTRACT

After waiting anxiously for weeks, Annah finally received her personal reading via email on Sunday, July 16th. It was sent as an attachment and suspiciously included a 'no reply' notation, meaning she had no way of corresponding with the sender. She will probably never know who the author is. For all she knew, it could have been written by a psychologist whose claim to fame was telling people exactly what they wanted to hear, while earning a hefty salary. But there are the Annahs out there who would pay for just that!

If the sender wasn't so ambiguous, Annah probably would have felt more confident with trusting its contents. She positioned the cursor directly on top of the attachment's link as her thumb nervously hovered over the button to open it, using those few seconds to settle her doubts and fears about the reading in general. She finally pushed her thumb down, opening the gateway to her future.

Amazed at how in depth it was, over 75 pages, she found most of it to be abstract explanations pertaining to the art of astrology, a few pages devoted to Annah's character analysis, and a section on clairvoyance. On a rainy day, it would be an interesting read, but today her only focus was on how and when she would reunite with Lance. She printed out the entire reading and set it next to her cup of tea on the coffee table. She fluffed her pillows and nestled on the sofa ready to capture and understand every insinuation, connotation and direct reference on how she and Lance will live happily ever after.

The first few pages didn't make a whole lot of sense to Annah. It talked about overseas travel, some sort of transit and a project that would be a very important element in Annah's life. She wasn't making a connection to what it meant or what it had to do with her getting back together with Lance. She was feeling a little disappointed, having waited weeks for a psychic miracle.

Annah was anxious to find out what it said about Lance, so she fast forwarded through the pages, honing in on key words. Several pages into the report, her question had been addressed. Now her heart was racing and she managed to smile for the first time in days. She made a first pass, searching fiercely for the part that affirmed that Lance still loved her and wanted her back. She didn't find anything remotely close to that sentiment, or anything that definitively endorsed what she was waiting to hear; truthfully, there was no mention of a fairy tale ending.

Annah hadn't gotten the answer she wanted, but wasn't giving up. She gave the reading a second pass to try and better understand what it was trying to convey to her. It wasn't until the third pass that Annah realized it was more of an assignment. Annah needed to work on her own happiness before anything could manifest in her love life, with Lance or anyone else. She now understood the report to be more of a contract and as long as she followed its instructions, it would only be a matter of time that she and Lance would be together again.

~ Personal Reading ~

Your Transit period will run from 18 July until 28 September. All the dates of this period will influence you positively in one way or another. The end of the Transit is very important as it is at this time that you will put your plans and actions firmly in place and you will start to feel very positive impacts of this unique Transit.

On a professional level, I can already let you know that this Transit will be one of the most intense and beneficial periods of your entire career. This period will allow you to take off and make great advances so let me start with this first piece of news...

This period will mark a moment of victory and it appears that this victory is in direct relation with new openings and a development towards foreign countries. To be a little more precise, you will have a bright idea that you don't yet even suspect and this idea will become very important for you as it will be transformed into a veritable challenge which will help you distinguish yourself and to shine professionally. I can also see that this project will greatly evolve thanks to someone who you do not yet know, but who will play a certain role in this challenge.

I can see that this all has a lot to do with overseas. I sense that you will be in contact with new people from other countries and other continents. You will have to deal closely with other cultures and you should be ready to adapt yourself to another way of life. Don't worry too much about this however, things will go very well.

During this period you must be ready to play a major role. You will meet the people that will be important for your project and your future career. You will find yourself in a very particular frame of mind, as at the beginning of this period you will first of all feel a powerful desire to retreat from your otherwise active role in certain events, which have just happened.

The foundations of your project, and the challenge, which you are looking for, will be established. A vital opportunity will be offered to you and I can already see it has a great deal to do with foreign affairs. I think that this new proposition will come to you through a powerful means of communication and this makes me think of the internet. This means that you should think about contacting people abroad, through the internet, about this project.

The dates, which I have told you about, are not the dates when things will radically change in your job. These are the dates when events will simply settle into place, and this means that during this period you, will enter into contact with people who will later have a great deal of importance in terms of your career.

Another point which appears very clearly is a certain progression, which I interpret as meaning that events will not explode into glorious fruition right at the start, but instead will take a little time to settle into place. You will witness more of a 'snowball' effect. I have to warn you about this aspect of your future as a matter of fact; you are going to have to be a little patient and you must be persevering.

It is clear that this project comes from an idea, which exists deep inside of you. This idea is not yet mature and it is not yet the moment to reveal it, but the time will come. You should not worry too much about exactly how things will happen, events will occur quite naturally. I have also spoken to you about an encounter which will have a certain importance for you concerning this project. This encounter will even be the vital moment that kick-starts the evolution, so you should be very active and ready to seize any opportunity which comes your way. Above all it is important that you make yourself available to contact a great deal of people and pay attention to how and why you made these contacts. You will receive a number of very positive feedbacks from people, notes of appreciation in fact, following the innovations you will make.

During this period your sense of observation will be extremely stimulated, to such a point that you will be attentive to the slightest detail. This will be an important attribute as your heightened sense of observation will help you push your career in the direction you want it to go in.

I would recommend that you do not worry too much about your immediate future because your planets will simply show you the right way to go. You will react instinctively in just the right manner and your attention to detail will be developed without you needing to force yourself to make any great effort. You can be entirely confident that during this period your intellect will be alert, sharp and constantly active and you will be able to seize precisely the correct opportunities at just the right time.

Your configuration also counsels you will come to terms with certain aspects of your personality. There seems to have been one single element which has prevented you from entering into the higher spheres of power and I can see that you have been relegated to the ranks of the forgotten for a certain time now, but here is a chance for you to show everyone just what you are made of!

It is a little as if a superior force watches over our intentions and over our actions and its only role is to immediately pay us what we deserve to receive. How can you doubt this magic in our lives? In other words, you have invested yourself in your career for a number of years now and now you will finally have the opportunity to harvest the fruits of your labors!

I have explained to you that you should expect some important changes as far as your professional life is concerned but you can also expect changes in your love-life. You will reach a major turning point and begin a brand-new chapter in your life. This will be a period of revelation and you will understand a number of things about your life.

You will reach a point where you will feel entirely fulfilled and very happy, particularly as far as your love-life is concerned. I can see that you are going to have to get through a sort of mourning for your ex-partner because even though something will be recreated with this person in the future, it will be very different from the relationship you have lived together in the past. You need to get through your mourning because until you do, you will not be able to construct anything at all with anyone, including this person. It will be entirely up to you to make the right choices at just the right moment to change your life and get back the happiness which you seem to have lost.

It is between the 13 August and the 18 August dates that you will make a very important decision about your love-life. The decision you will make will be crowned with success and it will permit you to reach an important turning point in your life. Your ex-partner is clearly associated with this decision. You alone will be able to decide exactly what role this person will play in your future when you reach this particular moment.

You will not know until the moment that these dates occur what will be the correct decision to make. You will need to find the solution, which is deep inside of you. Here is what you should do to get the greatest chance over on your side, if your final decision will be to return with your ex-partner.

First of all, do not try to contact this person before the Transit. This is very important. You must respect this agreement with yourself, even if this does seem to be quite hard to do. If you do encounter your ex-partner during this period by chance or by error don't worry because you will not have set up the meeting.

I know that recently you have had such thoughts as 'I can never be happy until my partner comes back to me', 'My partner is the only person I could ever love', and 'I want my partner to be here with me now so that I can feel good'. Believe it or not, it is important for your partner to feel challenged and that an effort must be made to get close to you again. I am going to ask you to make a little effort for just a few seconds be very honest with yourself. Admit to yourself that you don't need your ex in your life anymore and that you can live very well without this person, and there are a number of other very charming people who could suit you just as well. This is a truth, which your uncon-scious recognizes very well, no matter what you may con-sciously believe. If you don't have something, which you desire, you will feel disappointed. However, you will not be as devastated as you would be if you lacked something which you firmly believe that you need. It is very important that you get things into context as you do have a tendency to want exactly what you cannot have. I know that because you cannot have this person close to you at the moment, your feelings are unclear and this makes you vulnerable.

Society reassures us that feeling a very intense grief after breaking up with someone is entirely normal and that it should always be this way, however, those people who do not force themselves to feel this way do actually feel a lot better a few months later.

I want you to start doing some sport or some form of exercise, either daily or as often as you can. This is important and you must take this seriously. Your new discipline will help you with the transformations you need to make, and emotionally and physically it will bring you a lot more than you suspect. You need to feel good deep within yourself to give yourself the maximum chance possible to make something good out of this period.

Now I want to tell you how you should act when you meet your ex-partner. First of all you need to keep the mystery alive. When you meet your ex again this person is going to want to talk about themselves, and you should let them do so for most of this meeting. Keep your side of things vague and mysterious. Bear in mind that 'sometimes, less is more'.

You are going to have to create a very exciting atmosphere, but limit the amount of time you are going to spend together during this encounter. Above all, if things appear to be going well or if you want things to go further, don't prolong the encounter any longer than you should. You should also not go back into the past, do not talk about your past life together. This is a very important point, but if you do need to talk about past things, avoid negative elements and leave what is from the past in the past. This is why it is important for you to prepare yourself well before this period, so that you can be on good form, happy and relaxed. Try not to appear sad in front of your ex, especially not to get this person back close to you. This will not have a positive impact, quite the contrary in fact. Show your happiness!

Now something else very important: when you get in contact with your ex-partner to set up some sort of encounter, for this to work well you must not appear to be too needy. Propose a specific activity for this meeting, the more specific you can be, the more successful you will also be. Don't put any pressure on this person, even if your ex initially refuses an encounter. We will look later on at how to deal with this, if this is the case. This encounter should be, above all, just to have fun. Your ex will be prepared for you to react in a certain way and the mere fact that you do not enter into one of these roles will surprise this person and have a much greater impact than anything else you could do.

At the end of this encounter, don't plan on anything else, just see how it goes and don't make any plans for another meeting. Whilst you two talk, you must make sure never to go back and discuss your separation and the reasons behind your break-up, nor anything else which could be negative. As I have already told you, I have foreseen astrologically that you will get back in contact with this person. It is by phone that you will organize this meeting with your ex. What I can tell you at this stage, in my explications, is that if you follow the advice which I have given you to prepare yourself at the precise moment that you call your ex, this person will feel that you are a new person entirely.

But let's get back to the possibility that your ex refuses to meet up with you. The first thing which you must remember is not to react in a negative manner. Simply say 'OK' and gently change the subject. Don't even ask why you have been turned down, simply change the conversation and finish your phone call in a joyful and positive manner.

I can also foresee that your romantic future is very positive and that it will take an entirely new and exciting direction following this Transit. Bear this in mind and remember what I have told you if your partner does initially refuse this encounter, after a couple of trials turn your attention to someone else. It is clearly marked in your configuration that you will live through a dramatically positive change in your life and you will be headed straight for emotional happiness and satisfaction.

THE TRANSIT

Annah read her personal reading, which she refers to as, 'The Contract,' over and over again. She wanted to make sure she correctly interpreted every word, phrase, and meaning. As much as her sights, initially, were only set on her love life, she understood the importance of working on her physical, mental and emotional health in preparation for the much anticipated encounter.

The hardest thing for Annah to wrap her mind around was that she had to immediately cease communication with Lance. It wasn't as if she had planned to call him, it was the fact that even if she wanted to, she couldn't; any contact was now taboo. The Contract hit the nail when it mentioned Annah having a tendency to want exactly what she couldn't have.

And what she couldn't have, was Lance in her life.

The Contract emphasized an inclination towards foreign business and overseas travel. Innately, Annah is an analytical thinker and loves to solve puzzles and cryptic messages, so deciphering how this would play into her life was a challenge she happily accepted.

She thought for hours, concocting different scenarios, trying to make sure the components of each theory resonated with the words of the reading. Finally, she came up with a viable concept that she felt was entirely feasible.

Annah's company was in its final stages of launching its product in South America, and had already established its international headquarters in Brazil. So that would most definitely satisfy the notion of development in a foreign country. Additionally, the office buzz was that a team would be developed, from the IT department, to head up the installation and training—that would satisfy the overseas travel if Annah were selected, as well as dealing with people on another continent; adapting to another culture; and the opportunity to shine professionally.

The only other scenario, considering Annah's fragile condition, was that if she had a brief moment of indiscretion. Would she question the value and meaning of her life? Her world had definitely changed; life as she knew it had been snuffed out like a candle flame whose wick had met its end. Would she end her life so that her loved ones wouldn't be burdened by the skeleton of a person she had become? Her restless and nomadic soul would then be free to travel to all the exotic places she had only dreamt about when she was alive. But taking her own life was not an option for Annah, at least not now, and hopefully not ever.

Annah was bewildered as to why she was investing so much of her energy in a report prepared by someone she had never met—a person who couldn't possibly know anything about her; she had only provided basic information when she ordered the reading. But for some peculiar reason, one that she can't begin to explain, she trusted her gut that this was a divine intervention. In Annah's world, there are no coincidences; this all had to be happening for a reason. Besides, the reading was too personal for it to be random or generic. She had nothing to lose by putting her faith in whoever took on the task of guiding her through this rough patch.

The Contract referred to some sort of transit. The word *transit* is usually associated with a means of transportation which, referring back to Annah's theory on overseas travel, the mode of transport would be an airplane.

It couldn't be that simple, could it?
If it was that cut and dry, why wouldn't the astrologer have explained it that way?

Annah delved further into the translation of the term *transit* and found, in astrological terms, to be defined as, "A trend of circumstances, which are predicted based on the movement of the planets relative to certain traits in your natal chart. When the two are in a favorable position, they place favorable opportunities directly in one's path."

There are many skeptics who don't buy into astrological readings or horoscopes. They feel that predictions are given in general terms and could encompass a wide range of possibilities and situations that could occur in anyone's life. Annah was among those skeptics until recently. In fact, she felt this personal reading was unlike anything she had ever read before. It was more precise and actually gave detailed instruction, ensuring she would get the most out of this favorable opportunity. She couldn't help but feel elated. Some spiritual force in the great beyond had realized it was her time to reap the harvest of the beneficence she had been cultivating her entire life.

Her problem, as she saw it, was to make sure she wasn't doing anything to ensure that the events in her life were molded to the ideas expressed in the reading. There would be a tendency to do that, she realized.

Annah became intrigued by the entire transiting concept. In the study of astronomy, it appears to be intrinsic, yet so foreign to the average person. She began to read an article she stumbled across devoted to transits, specifically the subject of *transiting planetary returns*.

"A planetary return is when a transiting planet returns to the precise position it was in, in the zodiac, at the moment of your birth. In short, it means that the planet is beginning a new cycle and in turn a new cycle begins a person's life—a rebirth."

If she understood this correctly, the transit referred to in the reading was actually a transiting planetary return. This was all helpful in understanding the basis of her analysis. She was at the threshold of a new beginning, but she had to shed her outdated way of living and out-moded ways of thinking—a metamorphosis if you will; the caterpillar encased in its cocoon awaiting its emergence to a beautiful butterfly. She was feeling more at ease with this new knowledge, but still a little apprehensive, or more so intimidated, by the unfamiliar and understandably horrified by the unknown.

With that being said, she began to understand, on a superficial level, how trends or patterns can be determined. That accounts for the specific dates and favorable aspects outlined in her reading. What she couldn't fathom, however, was how it categorically translated to the most recent events that had just occurred in her life. For instance, The Contract mentioned that at the beginning of the transit, she would feel a powerful desire to retreat from certain events that had just occurred in her life. She indeed withdrew from every area of her life as a result of the mental breakdown.

Nonetheless, with The Contract in her possession, it was up to her to strictly adhere to its guiding principles, which she knew were dictated by the alignment of her planets. The transit was upon her and the rebirth had begun. Knowing she had the endorsement of the universe, she felt an inner strength that she had never felt before. She would use this power to meet her challenges with rigorous enthusiasm and to prepare herself for the moment of truth.

With this bounty of wisdom and knowledge at her disposal, she knew she couldn't fail. She could now dispel negativity and displace it with a more positive outlook.

She would use every experience, good or bad, as a lesson learned; obstacles would be viewed as mere stumbling blocks that were conquerable; if she fell, she could get back up and dust herself off; and disappointments were essential to learning life's lessons. This, she also realized, was a good plan for anybody with or without a reading.

She would become a new person—a better person.

THE MIND IS
THE MATTER

It was the day before her Transit was to begin. She felt sufficiently prepared and had read all the material thoroughly, at least a dozen times, but naturally had a few inherent doubts. If she had misread or misinterpreted just one word, there was the possibility of going down the wrong path. Detours were not an option! She knew this was a very profound commitment and if she didn't participate fully, it could adversely affect the outcome.

Annah wasn't one hundred percent confident about anything given her state of mind, but somehow she knew, or more so had faith, that she would come out of this unscathed. The Contract was now her lifeline, at least for the next couple of months. It was the captain of her ship, assisting her in navigating the uncharted waters ahead.

Although The Contract was a good starting point, she wasn't ignorant to the fact that she still had extensive mental issues to deal with. Her mind had suffered traumatically, which demanded a more conventional medical intervention to heal and restore those fractured faculties—a jump start, if you will.

Annah had been out of work for a week now, but was still in no condition to return. She contacted her supervisor to let him know she wouldn't be coming in and was scheduled for a medical evaluation the next day to determine when she'd be back. Most people would think that was a menial task, but to Annah it was monumental; the thought of picking up the phone and constructing a meaningful conversation was mentally laboring.

She was becoming increasingly unstable and felt at any moment she would snap; a helpless feeling of dangling mercilessly over a bottomless pit of hopelessness. She needed to create a safety net in case her mind was taken over by morbid, inconceivable thoughts, or lapsed into a fateful moment of despair. She began to write inspirational notes on index cards, placing them strategically around the house. That way, if she were to succumb to a moment of weakness, reading one of these notes would discourage her from engaging in the unspeakable. They were reinforcing reminders that her life was worth living.

She made effortless attempts to only think cheerful and positive thoughts, especially since her subconscious was adamant on sabotaging her optimism, fueling her mind with jaundiced and shadowy elements that we all have buried deep within. It was an incessant endeavor to counter this mode of irrational thinking because her attempts were met with great resistance. The unrelenting surges of negativity were undoubtedly birthed by the sublime monsters that only rear their ugly heads in times of vulnerability. She defined this feeling as fear—fear of the unknown; fear of the emergence of the damnable aspects that lie in wait, deep in the hidden crevices of one's soul.

Annah was developing a deeper appreciation for those with weakened souls; the ones who decide, when they experience an imbalance or tumultuous event in their lives, that leaving it all behind is their only option; the ones whose dark voices begin to speak louder than the more logical and rational ones, the ones who believe our indigenous, diabolical monsters begin to conspire, using horrific tactics to asphyxiate the sustenance from our lives. In this uphill battle, we grow weary and no longer have the urge to resuscitate our lives. This is what leads us to end the madness as quickly as possible. Annah wasn't going to let that happen to her; she had too much to live for, which was her driving force. She was determined that this dark monster was not going to impregnate her soul.

Could this be the challenge The Contract was referring to, to ward off the dark demons, paving the way for all that is good to prevail?

Annah went upstairs and nestled between her comforter and pillows, creating a fortress of protection and refuge. Her house was devoid of life—still, quiet and empty. All she wanted was to ease the tensions that were causing a hostile climate to ferment in the pit of her soul. As soon as she felt safe and secure, her tight muscles began to dissolve like snow melting on an unseasonably warm winter's day. Her entire body succumbed to total relaxation, the kind that usually accompanies a hot stone therapeutic massage. She eventually drifted off to a blissful, serene place.

Sadly, her utopia was abruptly interrupted by a strange and compromising sensation. She felt soft strokes travelling across her pelvic region; a gentle tingle, similar to what you would normally welcome in a more intimate setting. This feathery-light brushing traveled delicately and deliberating down to her inner thighs and slowly back up and across to her hip bones. It was a phantom version of foreplay, but Annah wasn't amused or aroused.

Screaming out would have been futile, so instead she closed her eyes, rolled over, and pretended it never happened. She felt tears welling up in her eyes and an acute shortness of breath. This supernatural violation left her feeling powerless and exposed. She felt the offending dark force was waiting for acknowledgment, but she wasn't going to give it that satisfaction. It took a great amount of restraint to keep from screaming out for it to stop. But, as cowardly as this may sound, she instead decided to just let it happen and act as if she hadn't felt a thing. Eventually it did stop.

Confused and in utter disbelief, she sat up cautiously scanning the room for evidence of an intruder. She wasn't about to openly validate this daunting experience, and her first reaction was to write it off as an over-active imagination, except an imagination doesn't explain the physical violation. There was no denying it—something was definitely in her room with her; a presence without a physical dimension; a ghostly coward that found pleasure in terrorizing its victim, while hiding in the shadows.

Several moments had passed before Annah settled back in bed. Determined to brush it off and get a couple hours of sleep, she wrapped herself in her comforter and forced her eyes shut. All of sudden, she began to feel vibrations travelling through every inch of her body, like electrical surges, using her veins as a circuit. This went on for a good minute or so, then slowly waned. Annah sat up and stared at the wall in front of her; she was frightened, seriously contemplating whether she should make her escape while she could or stay in bed and pray that it was over.

She opted to stay in bed, but to her dismay, the mysterious energy wasn't done with her. It then compassed her and laid an oppressive weight on her body. It became difficult to breathe. Annah had watched several horror movies in her day, but this was more frightening than the sum of them put together. It wasn't science fiction with elaborate props and special effects; this was happening in real time, totally unscripted.

The demon of darkness had found her, in this weakened state, and used it as an invitation to procure her soul. She could feel its evil run through her veins, replacing her pure blood with its dark, cold, nocuous fluid. Now, it was bound and determined to demonstrate its power, the power she was strengthening by giving in to her fear.

The personal violations, for the time being, had ceased but clearly the terrorizing rampage was not over. Annah began to hear a thumping noise coming from just outside her window. She didn't have shutters or loose shingles that could have dismantled or taken flight in the wind, so she wasn't sure what was causing it. She tried to rationalize this commotion by using her frail condition as a handicap, making her more susceptible to audible anomalies.

Annah quickly retreated to the lower quarters of her house, snuggling into her sofa to hopefully get some uninterrupted sleep. While she was napping, her daughters had come home and gathered in the great room. They woke her up from her not so deep slumber. She overheard their plans to meet up later for dinner, which they do from time to time to catch up on the current events in each other's lives. She rubbed her eyes and yawned a few times before turning in their direction.

"I didn't hear you guys come in."

It was as if she didn't exist. Without acknowledging her presence, and totally ignoring her question, they continued on with their conversation. She pushed her head into the sofa pillow and felt a wave of sadness come over her, unable to understand why they were ignoring her. She knew she was wide awake—so it wasn't some bizarre dream. She held back her tears in the event they were just playing a cruel joke.

Entertaining a quick and fleeting thought that she had died, maybe she had become an apparition lingering on in her own house. Her soul was displaced, from unfinished business as they say, so she was continuing on with the life she prematurely left behind. When she looked up from that brief moment of solemn reflection, the room was empty.

Where had her girls gone?

Had she just imagined they were there?

They didn't even say goodbye!

Annah was trembling from the devastating notion that she had died. She loved her girls so much and couldn't imagine not having them in her life, or them not having her in theirs. She insisted they were not ready to be on their own; that they still needed her. Continuing on her journey was the only way she would get answers.

AND SO IT BEGINS

The first day of the transit had finally come. It was July 18th and it began as any other typical day, except Annah was preoccupied with thoughts of her future. The unexpected can be such a perplexing beast. Her instincts were to take everything in stride, knowing things would play out on their own terms; in their own time. But Annah's active, fantastical imagination began to spin fairy tales that had her starring in award winning films, reigning as queen over a great country; and even becoming an immortal goddess revered for her beauty and wisdom—all of which had her living a happily ever after.

Annah knew that in order to get the most out of this opportunity, she had to first release all preconceptions and idealizations of what this transit was set to bring. She wanted to begin this journey with a fresh, unprejudiced perspective. She decided to begin a journal to document the events of each day, every new experience, and all the details in between so every memory was sealed in writing. If nothing else, she felt it would become a lovely memoir for her children to read and pass down to future generations.

Annah found an old spiral notebook with shopping lists and other miscellanea written on the first couple of pages. She ripped them out and claimed it as her journal. She stared at the first blank page as if her thoughts would magically transcribe into sentences on the evenly lined paper. Drawing a blank, she realized journaling is a lot harder than she thought it would be.

It was only a memoir for crying out loud! Not a best-selling novel.

She chuckled to herself for making a mountain out of a molehill and jotted down the first thing that came to her mind—the title of her journal. She dubbed it, "The Annals of Annah." Annals are year by year recordings of chronological events, so hopefully journaling will become an integral part of her life long after the transit has ended.

Now that the journal had officially been named, Annah was ready to pour herself onto the pages. She started with one word and before she knew it, sentences were coursing out of her like the raging rapids in early spring, delivering melting snow from the mountains into the rivers below. The first page, and a few subsequent pages were now filled and Annah felt better knowing her thoughts were on paper and out of her head. She could now reference them whenever she wanted, or needed to.

After an intensive writing session, she finally signed off for the night.

*July 18*th

...That's all for now. Until tomorrow!

The first order of business for Annah the next morning was her follow-up appointment with Dr. Oliver to discuss her mental status and possible treatments. To her dismay, her condition had worsened according to a symptoms checklist originally designed by a team of professors at Johns Hopkins University. And with that, Annah's worst fear was realized, Dr. Oliver pulled out a starter pack of anti-depressants.

She began to reflect on the many commercials advertising medications for depression. She felt the actors appropriately represented the symptoms: social withdrawal, fatigue, and loss of interest. The most disturbing part, and her main concern with these medications, was the laundry list of side effects, which consumed over fifty-percent of the total ad time.

"Side effects include nausea, increased anxiety, restlessness, decreased sex drive, dizziness, weight gain, tremors, sweating, insomnia, sleepiness or fatigue, dry mouth, diarrhea, constipation and headaches." Ironically, most of the side effects were contradictions of each other.

Annah knew she had to make a conscious decision to be strong enough to beat the odds and not become a fatal statistic. But, as she reluctantly admits, she had harbored irrational thoughts, fears and feelings; questioned her purpose in life; and had foolishly wondered if she was a burden to her loved ones and society. She contends that once a person reaches the point of questioning their existence, they have already began the process of resolving their indiscretions, internally, so they are at peace and ready for their premeditated demise. This is called the pivotal point. You are at the helm and only you can decide if you are ready to end your life's journey, knowing that once the deed is done—it is final.

Dr. Oliver handed Annah the four-tablet sample pack of anti-depressants, along with other prescriptions ranging from anxiety medication to pills that ensure a restful sleep. She stared at them, still very much in denial. She had always associated the use of anti-depressants with more severe cases, like for those who were institutionalized. The very notion of having been diagnosed with a mental impairment was more than she could handle; it was just as damaging as the disorder itself. The mere thought of someone finding out her condition spawned an increased feeling of dread, which only served to compound her already decomposed spirit. Annah broke down in tears.

In her weakened psychological state, Annah still questioned the use of medication. Her life had always been the epitome of organization and efficiency and she wasn't going to allow this brief, and hopefully short-lived lapse in normalcy destroy the foundations she had built. She wanted her structure back, her logical thinking back, and most of all, her happiness and well-being back.

After Annah reluctantly filled her prescriptions she fervently argued that if this disorder didn't kill her, the financial strain of her prescribed medications probably would. She had already fallen behind on her bills, and the amount of her disability check was significantly less than her normal salary. So, to add insult to injury, her lowered income had just been reduced by fifty dollars for the purchase of these necessary expenses, but hopefully this investment would get her back to work and back to her normal salary.

With great reservation, she threw the first of many small white pills to the back of her throat and chased it with a healthy gulp of water. She was now in the hands of fate, so hopefully the heavens were looking favorably down on her.

Annah wanted to learn more about anti-depressants, hoping for something positive to ease her mind and give her hope for the future. She was sure the internet would provide more than enough information on this increasingly popular subject, so she searched for inspirational stories from people who had used this particular brand of medication. She was interested in hearing their battles, struggles and ultimate triumphs.

Clicking on the internet icon, she found she was disconnected from the world-wide web of frustration—not the glitch she needed at that particular moment. She'd often expressed, with playful disdain, that modern technology would be the death of us all. Quickly, Annah pulled up a screen of all the available networks in the area. Five local networks displayed on her screen, Annah's being one of them. Three of the other four she identified as being close neighbors, by the use of their surname. The fourth, however, she had never seen before; the network name was *Wroclaw*. She thought it was odd that it was within such close range, but she knew no one by that name. She put it on the back burner vowing to look into it later.

After employing her tricks from the trade, Annah was finally able to connect to the internet. She began her search for those individuals brave enough to share their depression-to-success stories. There were only a handful of people willing to come forward and share their accounts, but she was grateful for those that did. They candidly shared their experiences with honesty and undiluted candor. But sadly, they all agreed that without medication, they probably wouldn't be here to talk about it; it's hard to tell your story from the grave.

She had read enough to resolve the issues that were causing her concern. All she needed was reassurance in knowing that positive results were attainable. Now that she felt inspired—she was ready to tackle this beast.

ALL ABOUT ANNAH

People often commented on how mature Annah was for her age and that her wisdom far exceeded her years. From early on, she knew she was slightly different from her peers. Although she was outgoing, witty and always found optimism in any situation, she possessed unique qualities that she felt differentiated her from the norm. No one ever knew her depth, and that suited Annah just fine.

Even though she had attended Sunday school and came from a God fearing family, she still questioned certain religious beliefs. It frustrated her that there never seemed to be solid answers to fundamental questions. She couldn't understand why we were supposed to accept religious writings just because they were written by the holiest of the holy.

Annah's ideology was, as long as you believe in a higher being, why do you feel the need to publicly

congregate and praise this icon? She felt the act of praying should be a private moment with heartfelt sentiment.

Annah's personalized character analysis, which was
included with her reading, was pretty much spot on with
who she is. There were several pages in this chapter of
the reading, but this abbreviated version captures her
essence—the deeper Annah.

~ Character Analysis ~

You are unconventional, even iconoclastic, in your
attitude toward religion, philosophy, and politics. You
tend to see traditional religion as a restrictive, meaningless ritual with little to offer you, and you're eager to
experiment with other, alternative pathways. You have
lots of creative, innovative ideas and you often feel that
others are unwilling to take risks and venture out of their
deeply ingrained perspectives and views.

You are very strong-willed and proud, but intensely
private and not easy to know well. Behind your quiet
exterior lies a great deal of emotional depth, sensitivity, complexity, and also fierce determination. You are
not a person who lives lightly or superficially. You want
to live passionately and intensely and are not averse to
challenge, danger, or to facing the darker side of life—
human pain and struggle.

You are very intuitive about other people and especially about their unspoken feelings and hidden motives.
You usually have strong, immediate gut reactions, either
positive or negative, which prove to be correct. You

approach life very instinctively and are not always fully conscious of why you feel or act as you do.

When you commit yourself emotionally to someone, be it friend or lover, you are intensely loyal and devoted to them and you also expect the same kind of unwavering, undying loyalty in return. If you are ever betrayed by someone you care deeply for, you are capable of hating and retaliating with as much fervor as you once loved. Nothing is done halfway. You are also very magnetic, especially to members of the opposite sex.

You appear responsible, conscientious, and solid—qualities which encourage others to take you seriously. You are unlikely to present yourself as more than you are, and this humility is often endearing, or at least appealing, to others. Even as a youth, you seemed mature for your age. There is youthfulness about your manner and appearance regardless of your chronological age.

Although you have very strong feelings and you often react to situations passionately, you are basically very tender and soft-hearted. At heart you are very gentle, impressionable, and receptive—a dreamer. The world of your imagination, feelings, and intuition is as real to you as anything in the outer world, though you may have trouble verbalizing or interpreting your inner experiences in a way others can understand. Mystical, artistic, musical, emotional and imaginative, you have a rich inner life.

You have great sensitivity and empathy with others, and you often sense things psychically or intuitively which prove to be correct. You are tolerant, forgiving, and nonjudgmental, accepting people unconditionally regardless of their flaws, mistakes, or outward appearance. You have deep compassion for the suffering of any fellow creature and often feel others pain as if it were your own. You sympathize with the needy, the disadvantaged—the misfits of society. You are capable of giving selflessly, living a life of devoted and compassionate service to others. You invest a lot of your creative energy into your home, your family, and your inner life.

You are more of a poet than a rational scientist. The language of music, art, or poetry is natural to you, and you are also able to think in highly abstract and symbolic terms. Translating your thoughts and impressions into concrete, everyday language may be difficult for you at times and consequently you may appear less intelligent or at least less quick-witted and verbal than others. You are intuitive and are able to sense what others thoughts and feelings are, even before they say anything to you.

You are extremely open-minded and believe that anything is possible. Intangible or spiritual forces seem just as real to you as anything in the concrete world. Your imagination and your sympathetic understanding of other people are two of your greatest gifts. You have an introspective turn of mind and may enjoy keeping a journal or a record of your dreams and personal experiences, or learning about psychology, history, and the inner workings and emotional foundations of your own life.

You have a nasty habit of holding on to past hurts, resentments, and guilt—and to keep such feelings to yourself. It is important for you to learn to forgive and let go. Casual, superficial relationships don't interest you at all. You are cautious and serious about love and desire a deep, genuine, lasting love. You are old-fashioned about courtship and love, and will remain faithful to your loved one in good times and in bad.

Beautiful, elegant, and harmonious surroundings are very important to you, and you have an innate sense of style, design, and form. Socially, also, good form and politeness are important to you and you instinctively avoid crudeness and dissonance.

You are serious about your ambitions, and disciplined, dedicated, and tenacious in pursuing your objectives. You are hard-working and capable of foregoing immediate comfort in order to achieve your long-range goals. You are not a gambler when it comes to attaining your goals; you depend on your own efforts and perseverance rather than good fortune. Challenging mental work is a good avenue for your aggressive intellect.

You are quite passionate, love children, and are inclined to wish for a large family. Your ambitions in life may have a spiritual component—based on a concern for social betterment or humanitarian ideals. You may have to overcome something in your background or personal past in order to achieve your long-range goals and ambitions. Overcoming the pull of the past is the key.

You are part of a group of people that are driven by the need to find an ethical standard and a clear sense of what is right and what is wrong. There is a subconscious drive to straighten out all the world's evils and create a world of perfect order. There is a strong feeling that you must extinguish evil in the world. There is a need for great transformations in attitudes regarding Good and Evil and will swing to great extremes.

This group had very intense psychic sensitivity and imagination. Your age group is very attracted to the strange, weird, and unusual. The sense of the macabre and bizarre is strong, and this is reflected in much of the music, art, and fashions of your age group.

Emotional depression, drug use, and suicide are likely to be relatively high in your age group. There is also a deep mystical sense, and Eastern religions and meditation are very attractive to your age group. You are able to do your work and take responsibility for overcoming your own problems and challenges in life, while at the same time being open to spiritual comfort, aid and guidance.

A good balance between being well-grounded and being receptive to spirit or the inner world is working in your favor. Enjoying simplicity and cultivating peace enable you to evolve and to work through your challenges.

It concluded by summarizing her generation as a whole.

The entire generation to which you belong has tremendous opportunities for spiritual rebirth and awakening. This will not be forced upon you or precipitated by unavoidable events; rather it comes from an inner yearning and a natural propensity to seek the depths.

GOOD VS. EVIL

There were times in Annah's life when she indulged in deep philosophical thought, like the time she felt the good and evil of the world would engage in a grand showdown for control of humanity. With all this talk recently about Armageddon, Mayan calendars and cosmic explosions, it does make you wonder how the world will come to an end. Annah was definitely inclined to believe the physical dimension of the world wouldn't end, but there would be a catastrophic effect on humanity from a contentious campaign of Satan versus the benevolent Gods of the universe.

Annah describes this as a supreme battle that began centuries ago and has been fermenting ever since, waiting for us mortals, through our values, morals and actions, to either strengthen or weaken one of the opposing side's power. To better explain her theory, she uses the analogy of a political election; two different parties with two equally different platforms, but you only get one vote determined by the views and issues the candidate supports. In this case, the more greed, jealously and materialism we exhibit, the greater chance Satan will win; but if we demonstrate selflessness, integrity, and honesty, we increase the odds for the beneficent gods to be triumphant.

We all possess both of these innate characteristics which are encoded in our souls at the time of our conception. We are born as guardians of goodness and it isn't until our experiences and prejudices come into play that the evil counterpart rears its ugly head and comes out of dormancy. Without our knowing, several attempts are made for an untimely takeover through tests and temptations. So whether we want to accept it or not, the devil has taken up residence deep within us waiting for an opportunity to emerge, at our weakest times or when we have sunken to the depths of selfish indulgence or self-pity.

The moment we question our purpose, demean our faith, or satiate our avaricious, self-serving appetites, our safe and protective walls are compromised, becoming keys to open hell's gate, which welcomes the devil with open arms. It then slithers in like a viper, camouflaged by its surroundings, intent on devouring its prey at just the right moment. Vulnerable and susceptible, we are taken in by trickery and deceit; hoodwinked into believing that the darker, shadier side of life will garnish us with glorious riches, control and fame.

What most of us fail to consider is that our greed, and hunger for power are major contributors to recession and destruction, and we don't realize we have the power to avert these calamitous events by staying true to our basic moral principles, and solid ethical values. We are all seduced by countless forms of temptation, which promise to fulfill our greatest desires, but it comes with a price—the devil has won and your soul has been sold.

*July 19*th

I feel I have been endowed with the task of restoring integrity in the world. I'm still not sure if this is the challenge The Contract was referring to, but if it is, I know I am worthy of the challenge—a strong person with good moral ethics. My only fear is that I may have to withstand a brutal attack of evil to emerge the victor of good.

Annah was afraid to fall asleep, but knew it was essential if she was to remain strong. As she closed her eyes, she tried to draw on positive thoughts and experiences. She chose to recall a fond memory from when her daughters were young. They would set up their kitchen set, complete with stove, oven, sink and refrigerator, on one side of the two-car garage. The overhead-type doors were purposely left open so they could enjoy the natural sunlight and fresh air. She could have watched them for hours whipping up gourmet dishes made of plastic. They would even pretend to go grocery shopping and purchase the items that were put back on the shelves from the day before. Once the shopping cart was full and the cashier rang up the sale, they walked a few steps to unload their purchases into the refrigerator and cabinets.

If only life were that easy—play money, recyclable food and hours of fun.

She woke up after two short hours of sleep, feeling swallowed up and defeated by the torturous psychological dungeon she was trapped in, imprisoned by disparity and gloom. Struggling to stay in a happy, content place, she cringed at the mere mention of the immediate road ahead. She knew that with one moment of weakness, her evil adversary would return for another round of unprovoked terror. Ignoring its presence was a temporary attempt to weaken its power.

Annah's plan may have backfired. Her detached approach angered the entity and caused its smoldering embers to ignite into a full blown conflagration. It escalated its subdued scare tactics to a formidable physical onslaught. It wasn't a foreign concept to Annah that your mind can play tricks on you when you're unstable, but what happened next wasn't a mind trick.

She sat up frightened, visibly trembling as her bed covers were effortlessly being pulled away from her body. She fought the urge to overreact; gently yanking them back and repositioning her body beneath them. Her first instinct was to stay calm to avoid giving this sick bastard the satisfaction of knowing she was terrified. Its intention was to frighten her and she was well aware of that fact. She knew it wanted her undaunted soul, but she wasn't going to willingly hand it over.

In an effort to preserve her strength and maintain some level of sanity, she hurriedly bundled her bedding into a huge ball, allowing any overflow to drag down the stairs behind her. Needless to say, it didn't take her long to realize she was too afraid to be in the bedroom alone. It seemed that most of the episodes occurred in that room, so it only made sense to get out of harm's way. Just for the record, she wasn't conceding, just increasing her odds is all. She felt a sense of relief just being in the living room with the television, radio, laptop, and other distractions close at hand.

No sooner did Annah find comfort in this safe haven that she began to hear very subtle, nearly inaudible noises coming from the second floor. It was like the sound of a marching band parading through town some distance away, only the instruments were unfamiliar; aside from the booming of what resembled drums. It definitely wasn't a composed piece, more like a musical commotion. And as moments passed, it began to sound more like someone was clanging on the pipes in her walls. She couldn't help but think it was just a clever ruse to get her to go back upstairs to investigate, knowing all too well what was waiting for her in the shadows—another terrorizing attempt to have her relinquish her power.

From that day forward, the television served as a trustworthy diversion. In fact, along with her laptop, they became her best friends. She was distracted for hours on end, with no concept of time, to which she was perfectly content. One show transitioned to the next, providing endless viewing of talk shows, sitcoms, news and movies. Surfing the web was just as consuming, a single search led to an assorted trail of endless links.

The daylight soon evaporated into darkness. She had almost forgotten the drama from earlier, but the more she concentrated on ignoring the goings-on, the more prominently they displayed in her mind. She knew it was waiting in the wings, using the downtime to refuel.

Annah had fallen asleep from either pure boredom or exhaustion only to be awakened around three in the morning, to the monotone voice of a late night show host. She couldn't tell you what the topic of the report was but she did remember feeling like this charming, tow-headed, handsomely attired man was staring directly into her eyes with the eeriest, most penetrating glare.

He began to speak directly to Annah, as if she was his only audience. His words were either incoherent or he was speaking in a foreign tongue; his tone was dark and demonic. Annah was still waking up, sluggishly becoming aware of her surroundings. She rubbed her eyes with the sleeve of her sweatshirt and pushed her overgrown bangs out of her face. Her eyes fixated on his awkward gaze as she sat paralyzed. His face had zoomed in, occupying the entire screen, and with an unwavering macabre, he asserts, "The metamorphosis has begun."

She wasn't sure what that meant, or if it was meant just for her.

Does this mean I'm changing?
Was I allowing the evil energy to pervert my mind?
Had it finally gotten to me?

Indeed it had. Annah was shaken, but wasn't going to cower to this diabolic malignancy. She chose to make a bold declaration invoking that these shenanigans end once and for all. In a trembled voice, she loudly and confidently spoke out to the ether, "Goodness will prevail. I will make sure of it!" She hoped her message was received because her intention was to cripple the entity's unscrupulous spirit.

No sooner had she made this proclamation that a surge of powerful energy surrounded her, and rapidly intensified. She had angered the dark side and it was unleashing its fury. In hindsight, maybe speaking out was courageously foolhardy—she failed to consider the possible repercussions.

In any event, she thought it was important to relate all of the happenings with regards to the demons to Dr. Oliver, who tried to get Annah to meet with a licensed psychiatrist when she was first diagnosed. But because of her discomfort with the subject, she wasn't quite ready to share with a total stranger.

BLOWN AWAY

Annah was able to get in a couple hours of sleep to where she felt strong enough to take on the day. Her first order of business was to get blood drawn in town. Having fasted for twelve hours, she made sure she was there first thing in the morning. She thought back to a time when you didn't have to leave the doctor's office to have samples drawn which, to her, was a time consuming inconvenience.

She walked into the clinic-like environment, innocently passing dozens of the already registered and seated early birds. As she stepped up to the next available registrar, a nurse emerged from behind a temporary, free-standing privacy wall a few feet from where Annah stood. The women instructed her to come right back once her paperwork was done. Annah didn't understand her exigency and wondered why she was called in before those that had been patiently waiting. She wasn't complaining, but if it were her witnessing this preferential treatment, she probably would have been pissed off. So she quickly disappeared behind the screen, hoping that maybe it had gone unnoticed.

As she sat waiting for the testing to begin, she thought, *what was that all about?*

"Why was I immediately called back?"

She did find it somewhat amusing, however, and composed a smug smile to acknowledge this peculiar turn of events. As the technician prepared the vials by adhering a computer printed label to each one, Annah had a numbing feeling that everyone was in on a secret that she was totally unaware of. She was getting the royal treatment, as if she were someone special.

As the nurse tightened the tourniquet around her forearm, Annah turned and asked why she was called before so many other people. Annah was taken aback when her inquiry went unanswered.

Do I dare repeat myself? She quipped to herself.

Annah opened her mouth to ask again, but was abruptly interrupted by 'Nurse Friendly', asking her to hold a cotton ball on the injection site. With her back to Annah, she placed the three sample vials into a small travel cooler, and replaced the slightly stained cotton ball with a small bandage.

"There you go—all done!" she announced.

When she lifted the cooler to leave, Annah reached out and grabbed her arm.

"Why did you put my blood in a cooler?"

"I've never seen that done before."

Somewhat perturbed, the nurse retorts, "It is used to keep the samples cool while they are being transported."

And off she went.

Annah dared not chase her down and trouble her with more questions...God forbid!

Annah wasn't sure if she was making more of this than was warranted, but was too tired and weak to invest any more time trying to make sense of it.

When Annah returned home, she was unsure if her lethargy was from venturing out or from having blood drawn, but it was clear she needed some rest. She propped herself up on the sofa with three large pillows behind her back, then grabbed another pillow to support her laptop on her thighs. Having read through a couple of trending news stories that were featured on the homepage of a prominent website, she found nothing overly interesting or exciting going on in the world, unless, of course, you are one to follow the private lives of celebrities, which she's not. She clicked on the horoscope tab to find out what the day had in store for her.

"You will be going on a trip. It will only be a short excursion, so make sure to travel light. Take in the nuances of your surroundings; you may want to reflect on them later. Take all the time you need, there is no rush to get back. Make sure to use the time wisely for much needed rest and rejuvenation."

How bizarre, she thought. *Another reference to travel!*

Annah couldn't imagine how the two readings synced up, and yet both didn't elaborate on where her travels were taking her. Her mind was already firing on one cylinder, so she knew digging for a logical explanation would more than likely exhaust her mental reserves. The only thing she knew for certain was this travel wasn't a planned vacation; she would have scheduled that in advance.

With that, her thoughts took a darker, murkier side of this mystery expedition that destiny so carefully placed in her path. In the absence of any other explanation, she concluded that the evil entity was going to be a companion in her travels, and perhaps the trip she was to take would be to his infernal underworld—the black abyss it claims as its home.

She could feel her heart pulsating through every artery of her body. The notion of a face off with the devil was evolving from a meager probability to a distinct possibly. Annah was now questioning whether she should abort this crazy endeavor before it had a chance to lift off.

Why was she so compelled to follow through with this anyway? There were no guarantees for her safety or welfare. Panic set in and Annah began to feel as though she wasn't at all prepared for this undertaking, or as enthusiastic as she initially was.

"Breathe deep," she told herself.

She needed to stop over-thinking what could be, or trying to predict the future; it was futile not to mention counter-productive. Everything needed to be taken in stride. She needed to curb her impatience and temper her need for a sneak preview. Assuredly, the answers would come in time. After all, patience and perseverance, isn't that what The Contract recommended?

Annah managed to occupy herself for the next couple of hours by indulging in a movie from her limited personal library. The already slim pickings significantly decreased after she eliminated themes involving romance, vampires, zombies and devil possession. She opted to watch *Charlie and The Chocolate Factory*. Not only are those animated Oompa-Loompas cheerful and uplifting, they are so the polar opposite of demons.

When the movie finished, Annah leaned over the sofa back to glance through her front blinds. It turned out that at some point during the movie there was an abrupt change in the weather. The sun was no longer visible and appeared to have been swallowed up by dark grey clouds. There was definitely a storm brewing. It wasn't forecast, but one of the idiosyncrasies of summer is that thunder storms pop up quite unexpectedly.

Annah got up to look out into the backyard. The densely leafed branches on the trees were fluttering about like a flock of agitated geese. Low-lying clouds blanketed the sky replacing all traces of the calm, placid blue sky. There was an ominous dread in the air. This wasn't going to be your average, run-of-the-mill thunderstorm. No, this one had the signature of something much more devastating. It was fierce and angry, ready to wreak havoc on anyone, and anything in its path.

She quickly turned on the weather station to get an updated forecast. It maintained its earlier forecast of bright sunny skies, with zero precipitation. Annah watched a little longer, expecting to hear that screeching alert announcing a storm warning, and the affected areas scrolling across the bottom of the screen. But there were no such reports.

She stepped outside to re-evaluate the climactic conditions, which were volatile, unstable, and eerily mystifying. As Annah stared at the explosive atmosphere, she let her imagination get the better of her. She felt as if the universe, particularly the Gods, were preparing for a cosmic battle. She felt the skies had taken on multiple personalities, and the clouds amassed to form crude images of iconic Greek gods; strategically placed in the sky. The panorama suggested the onset of a battle; an intense battle.

It grew darker, as if night had fallen midday. A sharp lightning bolt shot across the sky like a javelin being thrown by an Olympian. The claps of thunder were savagely booming all around—like the deepest pitch of a kettle drum repeatedly being struck during a tribal ceremony.

Annah thought, if this was in fact *the* ultimate battle, what would be the fate of humanity and why she was to bear witness to such a potential catastrophe. She shook her head attempting to disseminate all the crazy thoughts from her head. She needed to prepare for this storm instead of standing around spinning tall tales in her mind.

When a storm of this magnitude unexpectedly erupts, Annah makes sure to turn off the electrical box that supplies power to the pool. It's merely a precautionary measure, but definitely worth the extra effort. If lightning were to strike, the damage would be much more than she could afford.

She hurriedly scampered around the pool. Large pellets of rain began to torpedo down from the heavens and strong gusts of furious typhoon strength winds blew Annah around like helpless tumbleweed in the desert. She had almost reached the box when she felt a strong force pushing her towards the deep end of the pool. The once clear and calm water became rough with whitecaps slapping against all sides. Using every ounce of resistance she could summon, Annah managed to steady herself and avoid a disastrous plunge.

It was just as big a feat walking back across the yard to the house because of an incredible force opposing her efforts. By sheer determination, she was able to cut through this dynamic force. Even though Annah had never gone skydiving, she imagined it to be the same resistance you experience as you barrel down to earth.

Nearing the safety of her house, she began to realize the unimaginable horror of what could have happened. She was convinced the attempt on her life was deliberate. The gale force winds were supposed to sweep her up and catapult her defenseless body into the pool. Lightning would then strike resulting in her instant death.

Annah put all her muscle into closing the large glass door, while circumventing the powerful gusts that were reaching in to envelop her and pull her back out into the aggressive squall. Once she was safely inside, she peered out over the crime scene. It took several minutes for her to process what had just happened. Annah's deepest sensibilities refused to accept the fact that this storm had taken on a personality, and that she was about to be the victim of its fury. But if it was part of a grand scheme, and it had gone off without a hitch, Annah's death would have been written off as an accidental drowning, or worse, an electrocution. The truth of what really happened would have been buried with Annah.

She desperately wanted to call one of her neighbors to verify that she hadn't imagined the weird weather phenomena that had just passed through. But after thinking about it for a couple of seconds, she realized if it didn't happen, and she was the only one that experienced it, what would their reaction be? She couldn't risk asking and having them question her sanity.

She went in the bathroom to grab a towel to dry off, and in those few moments, all traces of the storm were gone. It rolled out as quickly and abruptly as it arrived. The mid-July sun came back with a vengeance—evaporating any lingering evidence of the damp and gloomy clouds that had just masked the sky.

Was this the trip her horoscope and The Contract were talking about, tripping into the pool accidentally? And did the phrase travelling light actually mean lightning?

When she realized she was buying into these outrageous ideas, she quickly reminded herself she wasn't going to let these goings-on influence her positive frame of mind. She decided to send a heartfelt message out into the universe hoping it would be smiled upon, "Universe, I am grateful I didn't fall into the pool, and doubly grateful I made it back to the house safely."

LEAD ME NOT INTO TEMPTATION

D r. Oliver offered his sagest advice, "I think you deal with the demons rationally and that is what is important to me; that is what will preserve your mental health and put things into proper perspective. Now it is entirely possible that these things have some root in your personality and predisposition and that's where, for the time being, we should leave them. Avoid telling people about them because the supernatural in any of its forms is just not possible for the average person to understand. Some of us, and one may be you, have gifts which enable them to deal with the supernatural world."

Annah walked out of her appointment with Dr. Oliver feeling hopeful. She was relieved to know that her symptoms hadn't worsened, but a little discouraged that they hadn't improved either. He felt it wasn't an immediate concern; nothing out of the ordinary, assuring Annah that a full recovery takes time. Even her dramatic weight loss, he felt, was common with this disorder, but encouraged her to get back to a balanced, healthy diet. He slightly adjusted the strengths and dosages of her medications and would see her again in a week or so.

Annah sat for a few minutes in the parking lot to gather her thoughts and regroup. She couldn't help but find it slightly pathetic that her biggest decision of the day was whether to go right home after picking up her prescriptions, or to stop by the market to pick up a few staples that would get her through the next few days. But, still feeling anxious around people, decided she was only going to make one stop, and that would be the pharmacy. While her prescriptions were being filled, she would pick up a few protein bars and vitamin waters to stimulate her appetite, which is what the doctor recommended. This plan seemed the most logical to her so she wouldn't have to make two stops, and once she got home, she could stay home.

With a plan in place, she started her car and maneuvered out of the parking lot. She had just gotten on the road when, out of nowhere, she began to perspire and became unhinged, clearly she was on the brink of an ill-timed panic attack. She gasped for breath and was nervously rattled. With both her hands clasping firmly on the steering wheel, she did her best to concentrate on the road and drive safely.

Annah glanced out of the corner of her eye, only to find that every passing car slowed down to stare at her; they pointed, heckled and laughed like juveniles as if bullying the awkward kid that didn't fit in. With her windows down, she could hear what sounded like mocking and felt she was the brunt of their derisive sneers. It was so unprecedented. She couldn't understand why they were being so cruel.

She stopped at a traffic light about a mile from the doctor's office and reached up to adjust her rear view mirror. When she sat back to make sure it was in the right position, she noticed the driver behind her. He was a balding man in a business suit, probably going to work. He began to gaze fixedly into her mirror, or rather, at her through the mirror. Annah gaped back, instinctively, with the same fixed stare.

Annah gasped when she noticed his eyes, they had no pupils or irises; they were completely white, bulging out of their sockets like two hardboiled eggs. That was one of the most horrid sights she had ever seen; it left her visibly shaken. She pushed the mirror up toward the roof to avoid further eye contact and drove off.

July 20th

I went to my follow-up appointment with Dr. Oliver. Nothing had changed, my symptoms were the same, but he didn't seem concerned. He said my progress was normal and that it would take a few weeks before I saw improvement. So I won't know if the medication worked until then...that's kind of depressing in itself. I have lost a total of fifteen pounds since this whole thing started. The funny thing is... I don't feel weak. He told me weight loss is a normal symptom and I shouldn't worry, and that my appetite would come back, slowly but surely. If he's not worried, neither am I...plus I went down two sizes...yay! But on the way home something happened that scared the crap out of me. I don't even feel comfortable writing this down because now I feel like everything I do, say or write is visible to the (thing). At this point, I'm not sure if I'm delusional, but everything weird that happens feels so real. Today, the demon was with me. I saw it, but didn't let him know I did. It scared me, but didn't let him know that either. What does he want from me? Why doesn't he just leave me alone?

Annah watched as night fell, alone and mentally exhausted, but dreadfully afraid to fall asleep. She feared another attack from the anonymous predator was looming because his previous attempts were unsuccessful. The fact that she outsmarted him by the pool had angered him even more, she was sure of it. Actually, truth be told, she didn't know what she was sure of. She felt if she were mentally stable, she wouldn't be entertaining fallacious thoughts of invisible forces threatening her life.

...I can tell you, when you are standing on the sidelines looking in, you can easily ridicule and judge mentally imbalanced behavior. But when you are the main character, living through this demoralization, you develop a new respect for those who have traveled down this misunderstood road.

Annah knew it was only a matter of time before the rhythmic percussions began to play upstairs, but she had become very adept at ignoring these predictable shenanigans. Her preoccupation, this time, was her crossword magazine. She flipped through the pages looking for something that wouldn't be too mentally challenging when, out of the corner of her eye, she saw something flash by, near the kitchen.

A couple of years back, Annah decided to give her house a total makeover. The split level architecture was extremely outdated and in desperate need of an update. The kitchen and bedrooms were originally on the second level, while the family room and garages were on the first. Fortunately Annah was in a good financial position to make the necessary renovations and design a two-story country colonial. Downstairs the garages became a kitchen and great room, and upstairs the bathroom space doubled, while adding another bedroom and loft area. These changes created an aesthetically pleasant flow and her house became more of a home.

So from where Annah sat in the great room, she could see the entire kitchen and out through the glass doors to the back yard. After a quick canvas of the kitchen, she found nothing out of the ordinary and chalked it up to the headlights of a passing car reflecting on the glass doors. She went back to solving the crypto-quiz she found, when she saw another flash. This time she was sure a car hadn't passed by.

Annah glanced into the kitchen then stared out to the back yard. She saw a wispy dark apparition slink by in the shadows. She turned on the spot lights that illuminated the entire yard. Leaning against the shed, in the far corner of the yard, was a black silhouette. It stood about six feet tall and appeared to be wearing a top hat and cape; holding a shiny, sickle-shaped object upright in one hand. She backed away several feet, hoping it was just a figment of her imagination. But it wasn't, something was standing there and staring directly at Annah.

It didn't try to conceal itself; it stood smugly in plain view with a wicked intent to scare her to death—and it worked. But instead of shrinking in fear, she flipped the switch to turn off the lights, and returned to the sofa as if she'd seen nothing. She stared down at the crossword in her lap to appear consumed, but deep down was scrambling for answers as to why she had gotten a visit from, who she believed to be, the personification of death. Even though she didn't outwardly acknowledge this revelation, the message was clear.

All Annah wanted was to settle back and enjoy a few minutes of not having to think about the weirdness around her. But regrettably, weirdness was the order of the day. She couldn't get past the reaper waiting in the wings. Why her? Was her time near? She was in the safety of her home, what could possibly happen there?

Her body became limp and weightless. Unconsciously she began to gravitate towards the butcher block stand that housed her knife set. She hovered alongside the edge of the kitchen counter, waiting for some kind of instruction or indication of what to do next. Her hand reached out to grab one of the knives, but suddenly retracted. She didn't know what to make of this, other than it being another desperate attempt on her life.

Annah began to feel a parallelism with a movie she'd seen some years back. A college coed named Emily experienced strange and other worldly incidents while alone in her dorm room. Her bed covers were mysteriously pulled away from her body; things would inexplicably move around in her room; she felt a presence or force pressing down onto her body; and she felt stalked by a dark entity. She was so frightened, she left college and moved back home with her parents. It didn't stop. Instead, it got progressively worse.

There was no explanation for what was happening to her, so she was seen by a specialist. He diagnosed her with having epilepsy and prescribed the appropriate medication. She tried to convince her doctor and parents it wasn't a medical disorder; that something else was wrong. It was because of her adamancy and increasingly strange behavior that a priest was called in to perform an exorcism, in the event it was a demonic possession. It was a controversial decision that was frowned upon and, unfortunately, Emily eventually died.

Annah believed in her heart of hearts that it wasn't epilepsy, but that Emily had experienced the same phenomena she was experiencing, the same evil visions and strange sensations that had been depicted in the movie. Emily's soul was dominated by evil, one that eventually took her life. This is why Annah felt so compelled to share her story. She felt no one else should have to endure such a terrifying demonic forfeiture. Her strength was gathered from knowing that if this information had been available earlier, Emily may have been treated differently and survived. Annah's only reservation was knowing that once she came forward, there was a good chance she would be taunted and humiliated for her ridiculous declarations, and didn't relish the thought of being stigmatized for opening up and sharing what she believed to be the truth.

There was a good chance she would be institutionalized for her views, especially since society shows partiality towards a prejudiced definition of 'normal' behavior.

...I feel strongly that the medical world is only book taught and cannot fathom the supernatural world or its control over us, mostly because discarnate possession contradicts the concreteness of traditional medicine.

THE ORACLE ATHENA

It was Friday afternoon and the neighborhood was bustling with activity. Most of Annah's neighbors gratified themselves with an extended three day weekend to either head for their beach rental, pack up their campers and head for a remote campground, or get a head start on their outdoor chores so they could enjoy the community pool with their families for the rest of the weekend. She missed not having an agenda or a set routine, in fact, Friday meant nothing to her other than another day of being confined to the house.

July 21st

You would think watching my neighbors going about their everyday lives would inspire me to get out there and do the same. Those thoughts crossed my mind, but I wasn't ready to face the world just yet. The best I could do was to hide behind my blinds and engage with the world as inconspicuously as possible. I stood at the window thinking how I missed being 'me' and down came the tears. It hurt to watch the casual interactions of my friends, knowing I was missing the gossipy current events of the week. Then, just when I thought I was all cried out, I cried some more. I begged that this was all just a bad dream and I'll wake up soon with everything being back to normal. The one thing I know for certain is that I don't want to be a statistic, so I have to overcome this—I will be victorious in the end.

The day was slowly dissolving. The humming and buzzing of mowers, trimmers and leaf blowers slowly wound down as neighbors scurried to finish up before the sun completely dipped below the horizon. There she sat, staring mindlessly at the four walls that were becoming all too familiar. Annah didn't have a highly stimulating day, but managed to expend all her energy. Now ready for bed, she took her prescribed sleeping pill to ensure an uninterrupted, quality sleep. After about half an hour, she was finally in a peaceful slumber.

…Even though I was sound asleep on the physical plane, I was fully awake in some other dimension. I know this is a hard concept to grasp, but that's the only way I can describe it. My physical body was still lying on the sofa, but the spiritual part of me was lifted and fully awake and aware of my surroundings. I was transported to a faraway place, which very well could have been my subconscious playing out the words of The Contract of overseas travel. I didn't fly through the air with oceans and mountains beneath me, nor did I sit stationary watching scenes pass before me. It was nothing like that at all. It was instantaneous, where in milliseconds I was transported to an unfamiliar place.

Annah stood alone on a rocky crag surveying the landscape around her. Her clothing had been replaced by a toga-like garment, similar to the ones worn by ancient Greeks—a white flowing frock, draped over one shoulder and cinched at the waist with a crude fiber rope. The loose tresses of her naturally spiced, raven hair cascaded down her back as poetically as a waterfall flowing down a formation of smoothly eroded rock, and the rudimentary tiara secured to the crown of her head was an entwining of leaves and vines.

She couldn't see her feet, but believed she may have been bare foot. The gravelly terrain would have been unpleasant with no shoes, but Annah felt no discomfort because she was hovering just above the sand and stone. She coasted effortlessly through a magnificent scene, feeling as if she had been cast in the leading role of an elaborate production.

In every direction there were crude, misshapen mountains, splattered with overgrown wild flowers; shrubbery that forced its growth through every crack and crevice in the mighty rock; and coniferous trees that grew on every stretch of fertile soil. Some of the massive stone peaks rose high above the clouds, into the heavens.

Just ahead of where Annah stood on the plateau were three fluted colonnades, several stories high. An ornamental stone molding was supported by all three, which held an array of square blocks with detailed carvings on each. There were stone markers, or possibly seats, randomly scattered on the grounds. Directly in front of the columns was a single tripod seat, also made of stone. Although plain and unassuming, she instinctively knew that a person of distinction had once occupied this noble seat.

She approached what appeared to be the stage of an amphitheater. As she went up three steps to the platform, the dilapidated collection of crude structures came to life before her eyes. She felt time was rewinding itself. It was like an artist introducing colors on a blank canvas one at a time. The trees became bridled with vivid shades of green; the mountains boasted contrasting shades of grey with metallic flecks that shimmered in the sun; splashes of vibrant and bold color painted the poppies, daffodils and anemones; the blue sky was complimented by feathery white puffs floating across the sky. It was definitely a wonder to behold.

...I thought, as I looked out over the countryside, this has to be utopia...beautiful and serene...the essence of perfection.

Suddenly, what seconds ago was desolate and unpopulated, had become fully animated with hoards of men, women, children and livestock. Annah settled on the seat of honor, as if she belonged there, and immediately a line began to form to her left. There was an archetype from every walk of life, from the poor and disabled to the rich and regal, and they all seemed to congregate before her as if she offered something special; something only she could give them.

As impulsively as Annah took her position of power, she called the first in line to approach her. An elderly man hobbled close, head low, spiritless. His skin was hanging on his bones like wet laundry sagging on a clothes line.

The canvas cloth that was draped around his waist was ragged and soiled. He raised his hand up to gently tuck his long scraggly hair behind his ear.

He knelt down and muttered in a hoarse and labored voice, "Athena, I come before you today for your wisdom. My herd is withering from famine, my crops do not grow and I can no longer provide for my family. How do I bring life to my pasture for my cattle to graze, and fertilize my ground for my crops to flourish? My family will perish without this nourishment."

Annah gazed into his eyes with tenderness and compassion, "My dear sir, the ground is plenty fertile. You have neglected your farming duties so your land has turned its back on you. You must cultivate with your heart and soul and your crops and pasture will flourish once again." The fragile man beamed with gratitude as he carefully stood up and went on his way.

Not every request was as simple, but without hesitation she was able to dispense the wisdom needed for every appeal.

July 22nd

It was barely 5:00 in the morning when I sat up fully awake and aware of what had just happened. I tried to recall every detail of my experience, right down to what I was wearing, the surroundings, and what was said. Without showering, eating, or even acknowledging anyone for that matter, I powered up my computer and quickly typed, 'Who is Athena?' I needed to know why I traveled to Greece and why I had assumed the role of Athena.

Annah got a shivering chill thinking back to The Contract.

I can see that this all has a lot to do with overseas. I sense that you will be in contact with new people from other countries and other continents…..I think that this new proposition will come to you through a powerful means of communication and this makes me think of the Internet. This means that you should think about contacting people abroad, through the Internet, about this project.

She realized that the overseas travel didn't mean physical travel and that communicating via the internet meant researching and deciphering her apparent out-of-body experience, otherwise known as an *astral travel*. There were numerous results to her search, so she clicked on the first one listed as a starting point.

In Greek mythology, Athena was known as the Goddess of Wisdom and the daughter of Zeus. Her birth was particularly interesting, as myth would suggest, she sprang from the head of Zeus fully clothed and ready for battle. Representing strength, protection and wisdom, she was known as a diplomat as opposed to a tyrant.

Annah read on for hours hoping to find something with substance to validate her astral travel. She finally stumbled upon what seemed more along the lines of what she was searching for. Supposedly, Athena frequently sat as an oracle at Delphi (a town in Greece), guiding the townspeople with her infinite wisdom. Delphi was known as the 'navel' or center of the world….indeed a very sacred place. Athena's trusty companion, the wise old owl, never left her side.

...I was doing some research on Athena, specifically why I sat as an oracle in her likeness. After hours of probing, I got up to stretch. I stood at the glass doors and looked out at the trees in the backyard. There's a huge oak whose lower branches extended into the far corner of my property. Between two of the very long and established limbs, on the inside elbow, was a knobby protrusion that bore a striking resemblance to an owl. I couldn't imagine how it had gone unnoticed until now. I thought my eyes were deceiving me, so I rubbed them a few times to hopefully get a better focus. It wasn't a typical deformed knot; this was an intricately detailed object. It looked as if it was carved into the tree. It was definitely an owl, not real of course, more of an artistic work of art. It was perched in such a manner that it was gazing at me or my house in general—like it was watching over me.

Annah marveled at this deliberate symbolism from the universe. She felt it served as confirmation that she was on the right path, either that, or it was a figurative souvenir from her travel, something only she would understand and appreciate. As with Athena's faithful guardian owl, this became Annah's owl of protection; her inspirational source of infinite wisdom. She didn't share her observation with anyone, fearing they may not see it the way she did. But to validate her sighting, she grabbed her digital camera and started snapping away.

...I can't believe I'm getting physical evidence of this journey. I downloaded the pictures and looked at them closely. The figure was definitely that of an owl. It made me feel confident that I was on the right path by finding the first piece to a very intricate and enigmatic

puzzle. Something very unique was placed directly in my path that was filling me with indescribable excitement. For the first time in weeks, I'm feeling a ray of hope.

Annah began to use her oracular gift to see the truth of who she was supposed to be. She had experienced these visions in the past, but brushed them off as flights of fancy; sometimes going to the extreme of idealizing her life as an orphaned princess, or even a goddess who was raised by a common family so that she could experience life without privilege, which is the sincerest preparation for her ultimate reign over all of humanity.

When she was a little girl, Annah would dress up like a princess and sit her dolls and teddy bears in a circle around her as if they were her loyal subjects. Her scepter was anything from a wooden spoon to a metal baton; her crown, a cone made from construction paper; her royal robe was a draping of her bed sheets and her high heels and make up were borrowed from her mother's closet and vanity. For the hour or so that she played make believe, you couldn't tell her that she wasn't the princess she was pretending to be.

...It was apparent to me now that I had to prove my greatness, humility and integrity by staying true to a virtuous life and overcoming the challenges that would soon be brought before me. In the eyes of all that is divine, I had to ward off evil, live a wholesome life, be compassionate towards others and share my wisdom with those who sought it.

Now that Annah had acknowledged who she was destined to be, she knew it was only a matter of time before her challenges presented themselves. From that day forward, she had to believe her astral travels would guide and direct her along a mystical path, while unraveling a hidden secret that she would soon be able to decipher.

That night, when Annah went to sleep, she traveled back to Delphi. It was bewildering why she had returned because The Contract gave the impression she would be travelling to different countries and continents.

Had she missed an important message?
Annah assumed her position on the tripod once again. The townsfolk were bustling all around her, searching for an empty patch of ground to settle into while anxiously waiting to receive or bear witness to the powerful words of wisdom that only the oracle, Athena herself, could dispense.

July 23

I could hear whispers, or more like the unspoken thoughts of the commoners. Smiling down on my congregation with compassion and warmth, I felt a sense of fulfillment. I loved these people and felt the love returned. I felt myself glowing as I gently pressed my eyes together attempting to burn a snapshot of this surreal image into my subconscious mind so it would remain in my memory forever. That must have been why I was sent back to Delphi, to bring that warm feeling of purpose back with me.

It was three o'clock in the morning and Annah was up for the day. She put on a pot of coffee and opened her laptop to further research Greek mythology and oracles. She wasn't quite sure what she was looking for, but felt if she was steadfast in her pursuit the answers would reveal themselves.

She stumbled upon a website that encompassed a good portion of what she was looking for. While sipping her coffee, she scrolled through the lengthy narrative that had her totally enraptured. Annah summarized the article and book marked the website.

"According to Greek mythology, ancient Greeks worshipped many Gods/Goddesses. They were thought of as personifications of the forces of the universe, (wind, thunder, sun, etc.). The Gods appeared in human form but possessed supernatural powers, superhuman strength and ageless beauty. In much earlier times, the Gods would consult with Greek oracles, known then as the keepers of wisdom. The oracles would forebode unfortunate or catastrophic events. This gave the Gods supreme power and respect and no one was the wiser. The oracles' predictions didn't always come true, in which case they would cleverly devise an alternate explanation.

"The most renowned of the oracles was at Delphi. The Delphi sanctuary is situated at the foot of Mount Parnassus; a holy mountain in central Greece. Anyone who wanted to consult the oracle went to the sanctuary. The oracles would also answer all commoners' requests, but not everyone had the ability to interpret their wisdom because it was often given in code. If the participant was worthy, they were able to unravel the code and experience a new level of awareness. This awareness was commonly referred to as 'enlightenment'.

"Most mortals sought divine wisdom but, like the oracles, their souls had to first be cleansed to realize this higher learning. Once connected with your higher self, you are able to stand up to prevailing religious and political views that deteriorate society and the world. We can then celebrate meaningful and soulful truths that are pure and earnest."

It suddenly hit her—a veritable piece of the puzzle that was staring her in the face the entire time. Going back to her mention of being a computer programmer, she would write code to create reports from the company's 'Oracle' database. You would have thought Annah had just won a million dollars in the lottery when she experienced this eureka moment.

"Remarkable!" she softly whispered, beaming from ear to ear.

...I can already see that somehow I am to convey to the world that humanity's contribution to its preservation, through its own enlightenment, is the key to its survival. So was this the lesson or message I was to take away from my travel? Am I being ordained as a present day oracle? Was I supposed to make this correlation or was this just a coincidence? Either way, I am intensely motivated to learn more.

Annah wrote down the words: Oracles; Delphi; wisdom; goddesses; and Athena, hoping one of them would trigger a stored memory or regurgitate a theme from her subconscious. But nothing came forward. She stared at each word individually thinking, maybe there was a code or maybe they were anagrams, when you rearrange the letters and they spell another word. She shuffled and manipulated the letters and still came up with nothing.

She was close to abandoning this theory when the word "Delphi" called out to her. She stared and stared until finally the revelatory moment arrived.

"Delphi!"

"Of course!" she chuckled.

You would have thought she had just solved all the world's problems with this observation. Annah was born in the city of Philadelphia—PhilaDELPHIa. After she made this connection, she felt another part of the puzzle had been solved. Chanting incessantly to a self-lyricized tune, she was ecstatic. With that being said, she now understood that nothing along this journey was going to be straight forward. She'd have to work through a tangled web of cryptic messages to solve this mystery.

...Reading about the oracles sparked a new flame in my quest to understanding the role I was being conditioned to play. I am starting to feel a genuine connection to Athena, as an oracle. I know I was presented with a rare opportunity and the biggest challenge is going to be implementing this radical idea to a world that has become avaricious, narcissistic and ignorant.

Annah leafed through The Contract because she remembered something pertaining to a bright idea and a challenge.

It appears this victory is in direct relation with new openings and a development towards foreign countries. To be a little more precise about this Transit, you will have a bright idea that you don't yet even suspect and this idea will become very important for you as it will be transformed into a veritable challenge which will help you distinguish yourself and to shine professionally.

THE BATTLE
CONTINUES

A nnah decided she would attempt to communicate with the entity that took residence in her home. She felt there was a definite association between her astral travels and its untimely infestation. She spoke out to the nothingness around her as if there were someone in the room.

"I know you are here, I can feel you. What is it that you want from me? I sense there is a battle going on and my guess it's a universal battle of wills—the good against the evil. I am not frightened by you, so maybe it's time to reveal yourself. With this ambiguous stand you have taken, I can only suspect that you are the coward that represents all that is evil. Prove to me otherwise. If we are on the same team, we can work together. If this is a battle amongst the gods, then please leave me out of it."

Immediately following her brave declaration, she felt a great energy engulf the room. It was surrounding her, penetrating her entire body. The tingling vibrations were starting again, only this time they were more dynamic and disturbingly intense. However, she wasn't going to let it weaken her. She felt it was an acknowledgement that the entity heard her plea; or that it was confirming it was evil, or that it was confirming her hunch that this was a universal battle of wills.

Annah now believed that whatever the reason, it was there to stay; at least until it got what it came for. Maybe it just needed someone with an agnostic view, to deliver a message to the masses of the world. But what exactly was the message and why was it so important?

It was a little after midnight, but Annah decided on a last minute journal entry.

*July 24*th

I know I am supposed to figure out something significant that will affect life as we know it. I can't help but feel that this malevolent energy may be trying to weaken me, knowing I will not take its side in the end. This journey, that I was involuntarily enlisted for, is to reveal something very important...I am sure of that. Some truth or secret is out there waiting for its' unveiling, but will this unveiling heal or hurt the world? I know I can only theorize at this point, so I fully intend to ride out this storm and discover what is so portentous that the universe would go through such extreme measures.

Annah was undoubtedly confused. In her heart, she just wanted to do the right thing which, at this point, was just to stay true to her beliefs and convictions. It also meant continuing on her journey and letting the universe continue to guide her.

When Annah woke up from an underwhelming three hour nap, she was baffled by the unprecedented turn of events from her travels. She hadn't traveled to Greece, sat as an oracle, or marveled at the timeless beauty of a mystical civilization. Instead, she was surrounded by a vast expanse of desert-like terrain. Although adorning its own mystique, she was unmistakably on a different continent altogether. The atmosphere was quiet with a subtle hint of dry air disrupting the loose sand particles that laid in perfect rippling formations as far as the eye could see. Some granules randomly corralled, forming miniature cyclones that danced across the sandy surface.

Standing before her was the towering bust of a pyramid in the making. Annah stood at a distance admiring the magnitude of such an ancient enterprise that was slowly coming to life. A caravan of camels plodded by, determined and with purpose; decorated with colorful woven blankets and enormous water bags dangling down their sides. Laborers emerged on the scene, donning linen wraps and headdresses. Annah noted the absence of women and children, and assumed they were forbidden from partaking in such strenuous physical labor.

Annah watched as this pyramid neared its final stages of production. She thought it was a little odd there weren't laborers hauling massive blocks by rope rolls or pulleys, which is how their construction had historically been depicted. In fact, the majestic pyramidal formation, which stood at least fifty stories high, started out as nothing more than a solid mountain. From the bottom up, thick rectangular slabs were chiseled and defined by crudely constructed lasers. The lasers were directed by a series of hollow copper piping laid out, on all sides, yards from the base. They acted as conduits of the sun's rays, creating beams powerful enough to cut through the dense and seemingly impenetrable granite rock. She marveled at this technique that was so simple, but made so much sense.

"Had history gotten this all wrong?" she questioned.

"Were these conical masterpieces actually made from existing rock formations, carved out by such sophisticated, yet primitive laser technology?"

In her apparitional state, Annah was able to maneuver through the hordes of workers with ease. Drifting to the base of this architectural wonder, she discovered an entryway and invited herself in. As she passed through the threshold, she watched the pyramid evolve from crude and undeveloped to complex and fully functional, a labyrinth of ramps and hidden chambers. Rays of sunlight peeked through recesses that resembled windows; a collaborative part of the strategic design. The sun's rays, at a particular time of day, glimpsed through the windows allowing the copper laser technique to create inner doorways and chambers.

She wandered through the narrow passageways, in hopes of encountering one of the chambers reputably used as a burial site. Ironically, Annah began to feel entombed by the shallow passages and narrow walkways, but valiantly pressed on. There was an alcove up ahead. She ducked in and pushed open the wooden door, entering a dimly lit, dank and unbearably humid room that housed a vault made of solid granite.

The vault was nestled snugly against the far wall, and in the center of the room was a huge fire pit encircled by stacked, randomly sized and shaped stones. Emanating from this pit was a multi-colored swirl of smoke. It whisked up to the highest point of the pyramid, escaping through a small chimney. Annah fiercely backtracked through the convoluted mesh of ramps and passageways to observe the vapor spewing out and into the sky.

The sun laid peacefully on the horizon, preparing to bid farewell for the night, as Annah gazed just above the highest point of this monumental structure. She watched as the dazzling display of wafting billows began to take form against the darkened sky—literally taking her breath away.

Its arrangement closely resembled that of an eye: the outermost oval-shaped ring was rusty-bronze, just inside that ring was a variation of heather-grey that faded to off-white, the next inner ring was sapphire, and the innermost part was a solid circle of brownish-black. It hovered with decorous animation just above the opening, and looked out over the land as if keeping an eye on all of life.

She couldn't help but wonder if she was sent back in time to jolt her subconscious memories; to recapture all that was forgotten or stored within her?

As much as she would have liked to stay a little longer, the images of this ancient Egyptian civilization began to blur, and she was transported back to her physical body.

She now faced the laborious task of finding a connection between the oracles at Delphi and the great pyramids in Egypt. It was after midnight, but her inquisitive nature got the better of her, so she consulted with her trusted knowledge base. Typing in the search string, "Gods and goddesses of ancient Egypt and Greece," she felt a lucrative starting point would be to find parallels between these two travels.

The first significant point Annah felt was noteworthy was that the Egyptian counterpart of the goddess Athena was a goddess named Isis. Having already researched Athena, she decided to concentrate on Isis.

In ancient Egypt, Isis was the goddess of wisdom, and was also known as the Mother Goddess. Annah noted the first common thread—they were both goddesses of wisdom in their respective countries. This was a very significant discovery, wisdom being the prominent theme. She read on to acquire as much information as she could on the myths and legends surrounding the life of Isis.

As myth would illustrate, Isis married her brother Osiris (apparently incest was commonplace in ancient times in order to retain the bloodline of the gods). The siblings, Isis and Osiris, became the King and Queen of Egypt. The third sibling, brother Set, became jealous of the power Osiris possessed. So Set devised a plan to take over the throne. He designed an ornate coffin premeasured to only fit Osiris, then tricked him by telling him to lie in it; Set then nailed it shut with his brother still alive inside. With the help of a few of his men, the coffin was carried down to the Nile River and tossed in. The current quickly took it away and it eventually ended up on the banks in a land called Byblos.

Isis was heartbroken by the loss of her husband and eventually suffered from, what we recognize today as, 'depression'. In her unbalanced state, she sought out Osiris' coffin. She reasoned that she just wanted to bury her late husband in a proper fashion. After weeks on her expedition, she finally found the coffin and recovered his remains. Isis, with her mystical powers, brought Osiris back to life. This resurgence further enraged Set. The throne would never be his unless he could devise a way to eradicate the likes of Osiris forever.

Set, in all his fury, concocted a plan to dismember the body of Osiris. He cut him into fourteen pieces and scattered those pieces along the river, hoping the crocodiles would eat them. This way, the body could not be reassembled and Osiris would be gone forever—with no possibility of his resurrection.

Isis could not accept the fact that her beloved was gone forever this time. In her mournful state, she set out yet again to recover his body (all the parts), and give him a proper burial. After wandering for months and searching incessantly, she was successful in finding thirteen of the fourteen parts. The fourteenth part was his penis.

Isis was as resourceful as she was wise. She was able to bring Osiris back to life after assembling his parts, modeling a new penis out of clay. It was fully functional and they soon conceived their first child; it was a son, and they named him Horus.

Horus became known as the Sky God. His right eye was the sun and his left eye was the moon. He represented the mythical 'all-seeing eye', or as it is more commonly referred to, 'the eye of Horus'. It became symbolic of royalty and power. This eye is also used by the freemasons but is called the Eye of Providence, which is prominently displayed on the back of the dollar bill, in a detached triangle at the top of a pyramid. In Freemasonry, it is said to mean that all a mason's deeds and thoughts are being watched by God. In their belief, it is God's eye.

Isis and Osiris had encoded all of creations' secrets into their being. It is still believed today that those who carry the genetically encoded DNA can receive energies from the Eye of Horus and be transformed into Light Beings. Only those who prove worthy will be transformed and have these secrets revealed to them.

...I did more research today, this time on Egypt and goddess Isis. The part about DNA encoding had me stumped. Do I carry this encoded DNA? And if I do, what exactly am I to decode? I'm starting to get frustrated because I feel like I'm being given bits and pieces of information that are only making my head spin. Nothing feels like it has anything to do with the other. I mean there are similarities, like Isis and Athena were goddesses of wisdom, but

how do I fit in to all this. Also, I need to research the meaning of the all-seeing eye, being that I did see it in my travels…well at least I think that's what I saw.

Just as Annah was ready to put down her pen, she looked over at the name, Isis. She had another eureka moment, wondering how this revelation had gone unnoticed. She figured out if Isis were scrambled, it spelled the acronym of the first programming company she worked for, IISS, International Information Security Specialists.

THE AWAKENING

July 25th

I'm not sure if I'm on research overload, but for the past few days I've had an excruciating headache, like a hammer repeatedly pounding against my skull. I can only compare it to my worst migraine, times ten…no exaggeration. Nauseous and dizzy, I squeezed my head in my hands hoping all the pain would ooze out of any open crevice. I realize I'm already overly paranoid, but I can't help but feel like I may have brain cancer; or a tumor at the very least. It's making me want to take an entire bottle of ibuprofen just to make the pain go away.

Annah's headache had intensified to such an agonizing level, she considered making a trip to the emergency room. But following protocol for her insurance company, she called her doctor first for approval.

She told Dr. Oliver that she was experiencing a crushing, unbearable pain, accompanied by nausea and light-headedness. He asked that she come see him for a brief exam. He put her in for ten o'clock, which was two hours away.

To fill the time, she picked up The Contract, remembering it was sent with superfluous information ranging from the art of astrology to the study of metaphysics, and basically everything in between. She had hastily dismissed its importance, but now felt it must have been included for a reason. There was a particular section dedicated to clairvoyance. Its focus was on understanding the entire realm of extra-sensory perception and cognitive behavior.

~ Clairvoyance ~

The ability to perceive and understand objects
and events beyond the range of ordinary perception...

Clairvoyance is also referred to as remote viewing. It is often called the 'sixth sense' because it is the art of seeing with senses beyond the five we normally use. It is a faculty latent in all and will eventually be possessed by every human being in the course of his or her spiritual unfolding. Few people, however, seem willing to live the life that is required to awaken it. Some people become clairvoyant after a unique or traumatic experience such as a near-death experience, serious accident, blow to the head, or opening of the Kundalini energies.

Kundalini is best defined as a coil located at the base of the spine. Once it is awakened its energy travels alongside the spine until it reaches the crown chakra, which is at the top of the head. During this awakening there may be a fluttering feeling as the muscles relax and release more energy into the nerve endings. You may experience a nauseous feeling and oftentimes nosebleeds may occur because of the intense pressure behind the brain.

There are both positive and negative clairvoyance. It is the negative that is dangerous. It lays the individual open to possession by discarnate entities.

Opening inherent clairvoyant gifts has to do with DNA activation of encoded cellular memories, activations of chakras, raising frequency, balancing energy bodies, self-esteem and the ability to trust in what is heard and seen, and the present emotional state. Humanity is returning to an age of enlightenment in which we are all activating and we see the truth of our reality.

When the mysteries were still influencing the life of ancient Greece, a high type of clairvoyant was used in the sacred oracles. The priestess on the tripod was considered holy, and was cherished and protected from contamination of any sort. Some psychics believe that clairvoyance happens to people who are able to get out of the physical body and see by means of the astral body, or more commonly referred to as the 'third eye'. Medical science knows little about the third eye, also called the pineal gland, other than it being located in the back area of the brain. Resembling an eyeball, it is round with an opening on one portion, which is a lens for focusing light. It always looks upward, is hollow, and has color receptors.

The pineal gland has all the geometries and understandings of exactly how reality was created. Most of us lost our memories during the fall. At present, to regain contact with the inner worlds, it is necessary to establish the connection of the pineal gland and the pituitary body with the cerebrospinal nervous system, and to reawaken the pituitary body and the pineal gland.

The awakening of these organs can be accomplished when an individual devotes his or her attention to spiritual thoughts. When an individual has lived a moral life devoted to spiritual thought for a sufficient amount of time, this sets the pituitary body in vibration. This vibration causes the pituitary body to impinge upon the nearest line of force which, in turn, impinges upon the next line to it, and so the process continues until the force of the vibration has been spent.

The pituitary body and the pineal gland, two organs presently dormant in most people were, eons ago, connected with the involuntary nervous system and invested man with involuntary clairvoyance. It was the looseness of the connection between the vital body and the dense body that made them clairvoyant. Since those times, the vital body has become much more firmly interwoven with the dense body in the majority of people, but in all 'sensitives' it is loose. A lax connection between vital and dense bodies induces sensitivity to spiritual vibrations. The caveat being, if a person has this laxity between the vital and dense bodies, and is of a negative temperament, he or she is likely to become the prey of discarnate Spirits, as a medium.

As far as the growth of so-called extra-sensory faculties is concerned, humanity is divided into two general categories. Among the members of one category (the 'ordinary' people engaged in material pursuits and by and large out of touch with the spiritual worlds), the connection between dense and vital bodies is close. In the other category, that of the so-called 'sensitives', the connection between the two vehicles is loose. These 'sensitives', in turn, are also divided into two classes: voluntary clairvoyants, positive and actuated by their own wills and involuntary clairvoyants, negative and amenable to the will of others.

The involuntary clairvoyant has no control over what he sees or experiences in the other worlds. He is aware only of what happens before him, and cannot use his power for investigative purposes. When a person has this lax connection between the vital and the dense body and is of a negative temperament, he becomes a trance or materializing medium, and, when this happens, it can truly be said that his life is no longer his own.

It is extremely harmful for any individual to permit themselves to become so negative that his or her vehicles and faculties can be taken over by a discarnate entity. The entity can exert his or her control over the individual to the point where the individual can no longer exercise choice in any manner, but must live only as the entity wishes him or her to live.

Being highly sensitive comes with a number of gifts, as well as challenges. Sensitive souls are deeply affected by all aspects of life. They have great emotional passion, intensity, and depth, and are easily affected by the energy and emotions of others. A sensitive soul is a person of deep empathy and high intensity, with powerful intuition, awareness, and intelligence. They tend to be more sensitive to energies and environmental conditions such as lighting or sound, other people, excitement, and stress. As a result of these constant stimuli, they get easily overwhelmed or unable to cope.

Clairvoyance has the potential to free people from spiritual blindness so that we are no longer condemned to repeat past mistakes, miss new opportunities, or fall prey to seductive yet perilous illusions. Many spiritual truths will be revealed through the use of this faculty once it has become commonplace among mankind, as it is destined to be.

As it turns out, the Eye of Horus was also referred to as the third eye. That explained her travel to Egypt—to experience the awakening of the Eye. It was metaphorical, and now it made total sense.

Annah now understood the origin of the mysterious vibrations and was relieved that they may have been of good intent. She felt honored to be labeled a 'sensitive' and felt a dynamic power she didn't know an average person could possess. Now that her Kundalini energies had been awakened, she was definitely a force to be reckoned with.

...So the pressure, the intense pain, was my third eye awakening and the headache was just a by-product. I had a mixed bag of feelings about all this. On one hand, I was thrilled that I was considered worthy of being amongst the enlightened but, on the other hand, terrified that if I were wrong in my assumption, I may have a serious health issue.

Still, Annah realized she needed a professional opinion rather than relying on her own analysis which after all, could be influenced by so many factors.

She left the house a little later than she should have and was hoping she would make it to Doctor Oliver's office on time. Unfortunately her lateness was compounded by a detour off the main artery because of a minor fender-bender. At that point, her headache had returned and her anxiety was at an all-time high.

She hurried into the professional complex, which houses several offices offering different types of medical care. The aroma of disinfectants greeted her at the door. Any other time this would not have been offensive, but she already felt green around the gills. It was exactly 10:11 when she finally checked in with the receptionist.

"There's that number pattern again!" she quietly articulated.

She didn't have time to analyze its significance, but assuredly, it was dually noted.

Annah feared that because of her tardiness, she wouldn't be seen right away—which wasn't an option. If that were the case, she would have high-tailed it to the emergency room and to hell with protocol. Fortunately, she only sat for a few short minutes before she was whisked into the examination room.

Dr. Oliver immediately came in and took her vitals. He asked if she had experienced any head trauma, vision problems or felt achy because of sinus issues like an infection—she hadn't. He scratched his head, contemplating his next course of action. By the look on his face, Annah could tell he feared it could be something more serious than the average headache.

Annah decided it was best that she share her latest revelations, namely her astral travels, and the phenomenon of clairvoyance. The doctor listened quietly and patiently without interrupting, taking occasional notes. Then he locked eyes with Annah and said, "You are a very creative and imaginative person, Annah. The trick is to separate what is fact from what is being churned up by your imagination. Now don't get me wrong, it has been proven over and over in cases such as Amityville and others, dating back as long as records have been kept, of supernatural happenings. We simply have not been able, as humans, to prove these happenings. Sure there is evidence. That's what makes these cases worthy of scientific exploration when our first impulse is to simply dump them on the trash heap of dreams, or chalk them up to an over active imagination.

"The journeys you feel you have taken may either be repressed memories, maybe a lineage of souls, or the product of your research. Subconsciously you are living out what you are reading and researching. What I find a little odd, it collaborates with The Contract you speak of in your astrology reading. But I'm not worried as long as it leads you along a productive path."

Dr. Oliver calmly asserted as he wrote the referral, "I'm going to insist that you have an MRI done as soon as possible so I can better determine what's causing your headaches."

With his back still turned away, Annah felt the bravado to propose *her* theory on what was causing these headaches.

"May I ask your professional opinion about something?"

Abruptly cutting her off, and without acknowledging her inquiry, he quickly added, "At this point it could be a multitude of things. Once you get this test done, I can hopefully better diagnose your illness."

Annah retorted, feeling a little defensive and slightly agitated, "Thank you, but that wasn't my question."

"I was going to ask—what is the pineal gland?"

Immediately after the question left her lips, she felt like a total imbecile. She knew this gland had been dormant for centuries; she had read all about it. He's probably wondering where that question came from.

Dr. Oliver looked over at her as if she had three eyes (no pun intended) and hesitated before responding, "That is an odd question, but I will answer it to the best of my ability. The pineal gland is a gland located at the base of the brain which no longer serves any purpose."

He went on to add something Annah undoubtedly felt was a direct quote from his medical journal, or some other scholarly reference book. His answer far exceeded Annah's limited medical jargon, which left her feeling more confused than before she asked. Still, Annah wondered if she was the only person in this modern age that had experienced an awakening.

She quickly abandoned the idea of disclosing her unconventional theory and instead allowed herself to believe what she felt to be true. The doctor handed Annah a referral for an MRI to be scheduled as soon as possible, assuring her that as soon as he gets the results, he would contact her. In the meantime, she was to continue taking ibuprofen for the pain.

As soon as Annah got home, she called the imaging center and secured an appointment for later that afternoon.

...I don't know how to describe it, but I felt I was being shadowed at the appointment—like I wasn't alone. It's that feeling you get that someone is standing directly behind or beside you and, out of the corner of your eye, you actually catch a quick glimpse of an image, but when you turn and look in that direction, nothing is there. Maybe the predator, that was stalking me at home, followed

me to my appointment to make sure I don't disclose its dark secret. Then again, it could just be my emotional disorder causing self-imposed phobias.

Annah sensed that this awakening was posing a threat to the entity. Whatever this secret or forbidden knowledge was, it had to be so powerful that something or someone was adamant on keeping it buried. Her biggest concern was how to protect herself.

…Without accurate knowledge on this subject, I feel that maybe I am being tricked into opening hell's gate. There was so much information coming in, and from all sides. The more I learn, the more confused I get, but I still want to continue on this journey. I really want to believe in this 'third eye' epiphany, but what if I am on the wrong track? What if this is all just a diversion to some underlying conspiracy? I don't know why I insist on questioning myself all the time.

She refused to let the devil inside her head, assuring herself that she was on the right track and to stop doubting her innate intuition.

THE BEWITCHING
HOUR

With the MRI completed, and the rest of her day predictably uneventful, Annah popped a few ibuprofens and carefully placed her head on her pillow, hoping at any moment the pain would magically disappear. A zillion thoughts were bouncing around in her head making it much harder to get settled. But eventually, she managed to pull a single memory from her mental archives that brought her immense joy, the moment she rocked her first born to sleep for the first time.

She entered that tranquil place of unconscious solitude where hopes and dreams are boundless, and worries and concerns cease to exist. But as with most good things in life, they eventually come to an end. She was abruptly awakened only an hour into her sleep by the melodious ring tone of her cell phone.

It was Dr. Oliver.

"Annah, I just wanted you to know that your MRI showed no abnormalities. Are you feeling any better?"

"I still feel a dull throbbing, but not nearly as excruciating as before, and now that I got this news, I feel that much better."

"Well, if the headaches are still present in a few days, please call my office immediately."

"I will. Thank you for everything."

Annah was thrilled that the MRI came back showing no traces of tumors or other deviancies. For the first time in a long while, she felt truly blessed. Her headache had subsided and now, without reservation, she was ready to go full-bore on this journey that awaited her. It was time to stifle her fears and insecurities, to face life and all of its uncertainties, and most importantly, she knew it was high time she reclaim all that was rightfully hers—namely moving back into her bedroom.

*July 26*th

It feels so good to be back in my bed, snug as a bug in my freshly washed and line-dried sheets. I feel completely content, but have a gnawing hunch that this dose of happiness is going to be quashed by a relentless force that insists on lingering past its sell date. I know I will persevere. It just takes so much out of me.

Regrettably, Annah was right. The entity soon realized that she had returned to its nefarious den. A cold and dreary blanket girdled her body as if its intention was to squeeze the last breath from her nimble body. The powerless feeling and dread of what might happen next paralyzed her into submission. She had become a marionette whose strings were being pulled by the evil puppet master himself. He had finally succeeded in his attempts for her to relinquish control, at least temporarily.

The pipes began their less than tuneful banging and clanging. Annah pleaded for it to stop, but her cries only gratified the dark transient. Its intoxicating breath filled the room like smoke from a fire, consuming all the breathable air. With labored breaths and a weakened spirit, she managed to arouse the ounce of courage she needed to stand her ground, refusing to let this be her demise.

With a quavering voice, she audaciously asserted, "I represent all that is good in the world and will stay true to who I am. I will not allow you to soil my soul or taint my selfless heart."

After this proclamation, Annah took a sleeping pill and closed her eyes to shut out the world, and all that was going on around her. She knew this entity would stop at nothing, but her only defense at that point was to keep her wits about her and try to ignore its guiles. Her primary focus was to concentrate on her last travel hoping to either finish her business in Egypt, or be led to her next destination.

...I had just drifted off when I felt soft strokes running the length of my body, like a feather grazing my skin from my ankles all the way up to my neck. It was subtle enough to make the tiny hairs on my body stand up, creating goose bumps like those from a cold, drafty chill. I tried to stay hopeful that this irreverent molestation

would subside and allow me to get some rest. My mind is growing weary of these mental games, and not a day goes by that I don't think of those who submerge themselves in the darkness because they surrendered to the forces that left them powerless.

It was 3:00 in the morning when Annah began to stir. She stared at the shadowy recesses of her room eagerly hoping the sandman would take her for a few more hours. Tossing a couple of times, she even entertained the idea of taking another pill, but wasn't sure if it was safe. So she aimlessly wandered downstairs to find something to amuse herself.

She sat down on the sofa wondering why she was awakened at such a ghastly hour. Not that she's a black magic aficionado, but having seen several horror movies, she knew three o'clock in the morning as being synonymous with the bewitching, or devil's hour. This is a time when witches, demons, ghosts or other supernatural entities are thought to reveal themselves to mortals and be at their most wicked or powerful.

Annah felt something right in front of her, staring at her, mocking the fact that she couldn't see it. It wasn't a figment of her imagination, or an overactive mind playing tricks on her—she could feel the exhalation of a chilling breath whisper across her cheek. She did her best to ignore the trickery by remaining motionless and expressionless.

Sitting alone, in the middle of the night, was only causing her influx of fears to defeat her. It was time she go back to bed and at least try to finish her night's sleep.

She desperately wanted to leave the lights on, but knew it would only counter the subtle strides she had already made in eluding the beast. Once the lights were off, she opened her eyes and looked around. It was dark and she couldn't see a thing, which suited her just fine.

Forcing her eyes shut, she turned to her side, forced a contented sigh, and subsequently surrendered to a deep slumber. Her ruse, at least for that night, seemed to have worked.

THINKING OF LANCE

As mentioned in her personal reading, Annah was notorious for wanting exactly what she couldn't have. In this case, having Lance by her side was *all* she wanted, but sadly it was the one thing she couldn't have—at least not at the moment. It felt like an eternity since she last melted in his loving arms, shared an adoring smile, or heard his sensual, calming voice. It was more than the jovial and playful repartee they shared, she missed everything about him. She found it so hard to fathom how he couldn't feel the same.

As painful and gut-wrenching as it was, Annah was trying her hardest to abide by the guidelines of The Contract. It had been weeks since she felt such a heavy heart. In a weak moment, with tears rolling down her face, she cleverly crafted an email to Lance, a modest and sincere revelation of her innermost thoughts. She read it several times, making sure the wording wouldn't scare him off or give him a reason to not respond. But instead of sending it, she chose to delete it because she felt she was being tested. She passed this time, but wasn't completely confident she had the staying power to endure this long, volatile road for the next three weeks.

The range of dates when she could actually reconnect or communicate with Lance, were between August 13th and 18th. With that in mind, she knew she probably wouldn't make it till the latter of the dates. Call it impatience, anxiousness or just plain eagerness, but her plan was to contact him on the first date she was granted—the 13th. The sooner she could hear his voice, the sooner she felt her life would be complete.

Annah was second guessing why she agreed to put all her eggs in this contractual basket that was literally tearing her apart. Tears welled up in her eyes, and in a passing moment of self-pity she cried out, "I miss him so much—so much it hurts." She was starting to obsess again, and that horrible feeling of desperation was slowly reemerging.

*July 27*th

If I were to just email him to say 'hi', what real harm would that do? I wouldn't be groveling for him to come back. I would just be showing that I was thinking of him. He needs to know that I haven't completely forgotten about him and just in case he was wondering, he would know that I'm still alive. The way I see it, it is more of a cordial gesture than a needy one. I would have wanted to know that he still cared, and that he was still alive. Besides, if I wait too long, he may think I moved on and gave up on him altogether.

Annah still couldn't entirely wrap her head around the fact that contact with Lance was forbidden, and was frustrated by the fact that she couldn't ask questions or get detailed explanations from the unknown author of her reading.

...Why am I hanging on their every word? They have me believing they've pinpointed the exact dates I can reunite with Lance. I don't know anything about their relationship experience, or qualifications to counsel me. For all I know, they may have never been in love before, or experienced such a devastating loss. It could be a group of introverted misfits whose sole purpose in life is to make other people's lives as miserable as theirs...while getting paid to do it.

Annah thought there could have been a possibility she'd misread The Contract, or maybe missed an important key element or clause that allowed phantom calls or childish hang-ups. She shuffled through the carefully sequenced stack, honing in on anything categorically pertaining to the reunion with her ex-partner. She found the section she was looking for. It clearly and emphatically stated, "If you do encounter your ex-partner during this period by chance or by error, don't worry because you will not have set up the meeting...as long as the narrative does not come from you then it will not upset your plans."

Now that Annah had brought herself back to the point of despair, all bets were off in regards to not contacting Lance. Her reasoning, at least this time, was that if she called his number and he answered, as long as she didn't speak, she hadn't broken any rules—no harm, no foul. He would see her name come up on caller-id and call her back. Then *he* would have been the one initiating the dialogue, which was explicitly allowed. But, in all fairness, even Annah knew she was engaging in creative deception.

...Okay, so the phone scheme probably wouldn't have worked. It was time to explore other options. The Contract did mention, "... by chance or by error." I know where he works, lives, and most of the places he shops. If it just so happened I was on the road, in the same vicinity as his work, when he was leaving for the day, would that be considered by chance? Or, let's say I happened to go grocery shopping on a Monday, which is his preferred day to shop and we happened to run into each other, that's also by chance, right? I'm not stupid and I know it's not right...who am I kidding? Why am I stooping to such a juvenile level?

Once Annah dried her tears and stopped looking for reasons to contact Lance, she was able to regain her composure and think rationally. Aside from this emotional lapse, she was steadily improving her attitude towards life and love, and knew she was only weeks away from making her debut. So why would she even think about sabotaging her progress? It was imperative that she trust in the process and see this thing through to the end.

...Maybe it's best to find out if he tries to pursue me. Maybe that's the lesson I'm supposed to learn. Lance had to want me in his life again and desire me like he used to. I have to say though, being excluded from his everyday life downright sucks! But grasping for

straws, and spinning wild scenarios in my head, is only making me seem more pathetic than I already am. I have no control over the situation, and that's making me go crazy.

The glaring truth was that Annah hadn't shed her neediness or desperation. So no matter how she tried to rationalize it, a pre-mature encounter probably would have been disastrous. Besides, who's to say she just wasn't enjoying the thrill of the chase. Human nature does suggest that we tend to take for granted the things that are readily available to us, but there's something provocative about pursuing the things that are unattainable.

...I need to get him out of my head and heart, at least until the end of the transit. But that's easier said than done when all you remember are the good parts of the relationship; the memories we built together, his forgiving and loving ways, and most importantly, his innocence and naïveté that melted and stole my heart in the first place. He never had an unkind word to say and always reminded me of how in love he was with me...I was the center of his universe, and he was the center of mine.

Annah didn't want to think his opinion of her had changed. So, through her version of mental telepathy, she closed her eyes and sent heartfelt thoughts reminding him of what they had, and what they still could have in the future if he would just replace his bitterness with the sweet memories of all that was good. She just hoped it wasn't too late.

THE CAVE

Annah's finances were suffering almost as much as she was, and it didn't help that she hadn't received her disability check yet, albeit only one third of her normal salary. Suffice it to say, with no money coming in, she was diving nose first into a financial slump. She was hesitant, but knew in order to stay afloat, her only option was to withdraw from her retirement fund.

*July 28*th

I know I am going to take a big financial hit by taking money out of my 401K, but I have no other choice. How am I supposed to overcome depression when I am depleting my savings and security in the process?

The flood gates opened once again, sending Annah into a sobbing frenzy. She buried her face in her pillow, hoping it would somehow absorb her feelings of inadequacy and despair. It was somewhere in the middle of her meltdown that she decided to turn the tables. So far, she had harbored all the blame of the breakup.

...It was high time I stop blaming myself. I mean, I'll own part of the blame, but it's quite obvious that my life would still be in order had this not happened. This damned breakup was causing me so much grief. I should be resentful and full of animosity. Instead, I am hopelessly awaiting our reunion. What a pitiful mess I've become.

Annah forgave herself for having a weak moment, so long as she was able to regroup and continue on her journey. She was not a quitter and intended to fully see this thing through. Lapses and temporary weaknesses are healthy in the healing process; it makes you stop for a moment and gauge where you are and where you are headed.

With her head still in the warm hollow of her pillow, she relinquished her wakefulness to the unconscious state of slumber and was immediately swept off on her nocturnal excursion. Judging by the flora and mountainous ridges surrounding her, she knew right away she hadn't traveled to a previously visited land; the expanses of unsettled land were reminiscent of the northern region of the United States, perhaps that of Wyoming or the Dakotas.

She was in a field of bristled wheat swaying delicately in the night air, trying to get her bearings or some indicator as to her location. It was dark, but the moon's illumination was just enough to help her along her unguided trek. In every direction there was a range of uneven peaks that had an uncanny resemblance to that of a snarling dog's teeth—ragged and fierce. She started through the field towards a clearing, in one of the lower elevations.

Annah had become quite adept in being cognizant and astutely aware of the intricate details of her travels, so she banked every element of this experience in her mental journal; recording the particulars of the landscape, the location of the moon and the bleakly apparent absence of civilization. This was definitely no-man's land, whereas there wasn't a trace of human involvement or signature.

She ambled on forever, or so it seemed, until she eventually happened upon a dirt path. It led her to a grove of lofty coniferous trees that defined a range of massive peaks just ahead. She was just about to navigate the dense woodland when all of a sudden she lost her bearings, reeling, dropping to the ground in a lethargic stupor. Before she knew it, she was out cold.

When Annah awoke, she was groggy and lying on a rolling conveyance, resembling a hospital bed headed towards the foot of a mountain. Had she been knocked out or drugged? And, how did she end up on a gurney? She lifted her head several times and watched as images passed her by; it was as if she were watching a four dimensional movie.

As she neared the foot of the trail, she noticed a crudely carved opening at the base of the mountain. Her first thought was that it was an old and abandoned mining tunnel. There were steel doors attached to both sides that were slightly ajar allowing only a glimpse of the light inside to peek through. As she approached the entrance, the doors slowly opened. Bright lights glared out making it impossible to see anything in front of her. She was wheeled in through this narrow passage, then into an amply lit room. The heavy metal doors slammed shut behind her.

She slowly regained consciousness and was curious as to who pushed her into the cavernous room. She lifted her head to survey her surroundings. There were two figures looming at the end of the bed whose silhouettes suggested a human structure. They were fully clothed in green scrubs with white cowls covering their heads, and partially concealing their faces.

The hollowed bedrock cell was set up as a research lab. But not the kind of laboratory with test tubes bubbling over, or specimens in a glass jar. It looked to have more of a technological schema, which was a relief to Annah. For a moment, she thought they were going perform some sort of medical procedure, possibly using her as a lab rat.

There were two men sitting at an eight foot folding table that was set up as a workstation. A keyboard and computer monitor sat in front of each man, with some sort of antiquated radio transmitting equipment off to the side. Opposite the workstation were glass front cabinets housing a mainframe type computer system, complete with magnetic reel tapes used for storage and processing. The fact that the equipment was so outdated suggested a more primitive, unsophisticated operation.

"Mission complete!" was a transmission she heard come over the radio.

One of the two men, middle-aged, probably in his mid-fifties with thinning hair, and a perfectly manicured salt and pepper moustache, earnestly said, "Roger that!"

The other man, who was younger, sported a crew cut and was noticeably shorter and stouter. It appeared his responsibility was to watch the data that was streaming on his screen. He would then report any significant information to the commander, the older gentleman.

The covert nature of this setup, in her opinion, could only mean one thing—a top secret or conspiratorial mission. So it stands to reason why Annah was concerned with what they were researching and why was it being conducted in a secluded cave, in an undisclosed location.

A small congregation stood in one corner of the room, whispering amongst themselves. Although inaudible to the average ear, Annah could hear them perfectly. It was as if a hidden microphone was attached to their lapels and a receiver was mounted to her ear.

She heard one of them say, "She should be safe in the cave. No one will find her here."

Annah casually peered in their direction to see if there were any identifiable or distinguishable characteristics she would remember when she woke. They all appeared to be average Joe's, casually dressed in jeans and white button-down work shirts. Not one of them glanced her way; it was like she blended in with the wall.

...I tried to sit up and swing my legs over the side of the mattress. I must have still been weak, I fell to the floor...landing on my side. I was certain the disruption would have had everyone rushing to see if I was okay, but no one took notice. And, I still don't know how I ended up on a gurney. Maybe I was ambushed and drugged on the trail. As hard as I tried, my legs wouldn't cooperate with my efforts to stand. They felt like wet, over-cooked noodles.

Annah knew that laying on the floor, helpless, wasn't getting her any closer to finding out why she was there. She yelled out for someone to help, and hopefully tell her what the heck was going on. Her chivalrous knight, a man in a white lab coat, lifted her back onto the mattress. He moved in close, closer than she thought was a comfortable distance and flashed a small light into her eyes, probably checking for dilation.

"How are you feeling?" he asked.

"I'm groggy and I can't feel anything from my waist down."

"You were brought here for your own protection. The density of this grotto hinders the tracking of implanted GPS devices or identification tags. There's a group that calls themselves, 'The Dark Society'. This organization believes you may have classified information or know something they do not want exposed to the general public. They had been tracking you for some time and we feel, from the data we are receiving, they are closing in on your whereabouts. If they locate you, your life may be in danger. I can assure you, we are not the enemy; we are only concerned with your well-being."

"So how long do I have to stay here, in captivity?"

As with most of Annah's questions, this one also went unanswered. The man casually sauntered into another room and left her alone. She yelled out to him, "I have more questions you know." But it was to no avail. She was taken aback by his total disregard of her longing to know more. She stewed for a while wondering what she was supposed to do, and what their intentions were for her.

...I stared at the ceiling, which was as lackluster as the four walls, grey and morose, wondering why everyone was so rude. They don't answer my questions and only give me drips and drabs of information. There is an underground organization after me and I have no idea why. What sensitive information do I have anyway? I can't help thinking back to the morning that I awakened to a bloodbath. At the time, I thought someone had come into my bedroom in the middle of the night and performed some sort of surgery, maybe to implant a sophisticated data chip or transmitter in my brain, through my nasal cavity. Could my theory be right? At the very least, that would explain the intense headaches I was getting, but wouldn't it have shown up on my MRI? I guess my biggest concern should be who is involved in this conspiracy and whether or not I'm in any immediate danger.

Annah remembered an article she had read years back about radio broadcasting and communications from inside caves. An antenna spire was constructed on the highest peak of the mountain allowing a strong signal to be emitted into the vast unknown. So, with all the technical equipment in this cave, she was convinced it was being used as some sort of communication station. But who were they communicating with? And is this how they were able to track her?

Something definitely wasn't adding up. It unsettled her to think how she was manipulated into this cave, in the middle of nowhere. Why would they go through the painstaking task of ambushing and drugging her if their goal was to protect her? The nature of her capture definitely wasn't in accord with the explanation she was given. Maybe they were the Dark Society and had brought her to the cave to retrieve their data chip. If that were the case, there was a distinct possibility they weren't going to let her go.

Annah's only recourse was to get out of there. Having only regained partial feeling in her legs, a hasty retreat was improbable; not to mention the harrowing feat of getting out unnoticed. Her nerves were frazzled just wondering how she was going to pull this off. It was in the middle of formulating a plan of escape that she heard her thoughts echoing in the empty space around her. The once populated rock chamber suddenly became devoid of life, and any trace of technology had evaporated into thin air.

The steel doors slowly opened as she approached, which Annah interpreted as an invitation to leave. She scurried out and ran several hundred yards towards higher elevation, eventually falling into a tangling of overgrown shrubs. Although battered by briars and thorns, she used the down time to catch her breath, get her bearings, and plan her next strategic move.

...I looked down the hill I had just climbed only to find a solid wall of rock had replaced the door I had just passed through. Any and all evidence of the rudimentary communication center had vanished. I climbed further up the hill, through a thorny, dense thicket to the flat land. Off in the distance, I saw two beaming lights coming towards me. As they got closer I realized they were the headlights of what appeared to be a larger car or maybe even a pick-up truck.

Throwing caution to the wind, Annah ran out towards the oncoming vehicle. Her final strides were strained and heavy, bringing her to the brink of physical exhaustion. She stood motionless waiting for her heart to beat to a normal rhythm before converging on the dilapidated pick-up. It was still running, but eerily there was no driver. Quickly climbing into the driver's seat, she had no idea what she was to do next. She stared blankly at the road ahead; her eyes closed and her head fell forward, onto the rattling steering wheel.

...What was the takeaway from this travel supposed to be? I have no idea why I was brought to the cave. Nothing remotely similar was mentioned in The Contract. It had nothing to do with overseas travel or learning a different culture. It was just a bizarre dream that didn't bring me any closer to my goal.

When Annah lifted her head, she was no longer in the driver's seat of the rusty rattletrap; and the steering wheel, where her head had rested, was now her crumpled pillow. She made a conscious decision not to analyze this peculiar travel. It just didn't sync with the other astral excursions and, it wasn't worth the energy trying to piece it into the big picture.

Staggering down her steps, feeling mentally drained and out of sorts, she made her way to the sofa. But before settling in on the plump cushion, she grabbed her journal from the top drawer of the end table to update it with her most current exploits. After filling a couple of pages, the journal was now up to date. It was encouraging for her that with every word she wrote, it freed a portion of her mind to accept new information that was sure to come.

Annah replaced the journal in the drawer of the table and now, with only a few hours till daybreak, decided it was the perfect time to develop a fitness regimen as suggested by The Contract. Being all too familiar with the order of pages, she quickly flipped to the page outlining the importance of exercise.

"I want you to start doing some sport or some form of exercise, either daily or as often as you can, right up to the date of this all-important period. This is important and you must take this seriously. Your new discipline will help you with the transformations which you must make ready for this period and emotionally and physically it will bring you a lot more than you suspect."

Annah grabbed a piece of scrap paper to draft an outline of her fitness goals. Looking it over a few times, and making the necessary corrections, she was ready to develop an easily attainable and cohesive plan, which consisted of working out to an exercise tape in the morning, immediately followed by a walk. She would gradually add a second workout and short stroll in the evening.

...I gathered together what I thought to be essential materials like the appropriate apparel, sneakers, and small weights. Having these items ready would ensure a smooth kick-start to the new, improved and physically fit me. Tucked neatly away in my buried collection of obsolete VHS tapes was a workout video I had used years ago. It worked then, so I decided to at least use it to start out. There were a total of three tapes in the series, but I only used the one that offered a lower impact workout. It concentrated more on resistance training than body building, which I preferred. I didn't want to bulk up, just tone up.

Having a plan in place filled her with inspiration and hope.

THE MANE
ATTRACTION

The sun had risen welcoming the first day of Annah's workout. Enthused and invigorated, she promptly suited up in nylon running shorts, a t-shirt, and running shoes, then inserted the instructional tape in the VCR. After taking a few deep, cleansing breaths, she started her warm-up by marching in place to the cadence of her virtual instructor; clopping around the living room like a child pretending to be in a marching band, with her arms pumping like an animated drum major.

Annah knew she was shamefully out of shape, so making it through the entire workout, at least initially, would have been far-reaching. Besides, pushing too hard might have resulted in unnecessary aches and pains. So after about ten minutes into the active exercise phase, when her body screamed out that it had had enough, she fast-forwarded to the cool down and called it a day. She was very pleased with herself for following through with her commitment. The best part was, she felt energetic, upbeat and alive—and it was a great feeling.

After the workout, she knew she would only have done herself an injustice by burrowing on the sofa, which had become her normal routine. So she set out for her morning walk. The big decision was which route she going to take, and after looking up and down the street, decided it was probably best to let her aesthetic senses lead the way.

*July 29*th

It had been a while since I took the time to appreciate the simpler pleasures of life like taking a walk through the neighborhood and admiring the lawns my neighbors kept perfectly manicured; the menageries of blooms creatively arranged in their hanging baskets; and the neatly clipped and artfully shaped hedges. Each unique landscape offered a glimpse into its owner's personality.

It was that time of the morning when the automatic sprinklers had spritzed their last sprays, leaving beads of water on the blades of grass, and puddles on the uneven walkways. The familiar faces of the children, whom Annah had watched grow over the years, were joyfully playing in their yards and riding bikes along the side-walks, skillfully dodging pedestrians. It was reminiscent of Annah's earlier years—the long, sweltering, dog days of summer vacation.

...For most of my childhood years, I lived in Philadelphia. Our backyards were not big enough for elaborate jungle gyms or chlorinated, filtered swimming pools with sliding boards and spring boards. It was a row home with a 20' x 20' patch of grass we called our yard. My summertime luxury was an aluminum swing set with a slide and a citified version of a pool, the inflatable. It didn't have a concrete sidewalk around its perimeter, but it was awesome. I had become quite adept at improvisation. My knee-deep waterhole, on some days, was a vast expanse of an endless sea. Splashing from side to side with my arms flailing, you couldn't have convinced me I hadn't just swum the fifty meter length of an Olympic sized pool.

Annah had three sisters to share this small pool with, so they would rush out in the morning vying to claim a prime spot, which proved challenging at times, but they made the most of it. They would sit with their backs settled against the tubular air-filled sides, pretending they were living the lives of the rich and famous—complete with British accents. As they sipped wine (which was actually Kool-Aid in a plastic tumbler), they chatted about such extravagances as going to the opera (a matinee movie) and riding their thoroughbreds (wooden-poled horses). It was their luxury though, in its simplest form, and succeeded in occupying them for hours on end.

From time to time, Annah and her sisters joined most of the neighborhood kids in a more exciting and innovative way to beat the intolerable heat. It was called a fire hydrant. Some of the area teenagers, who the adults referred to as hooligans, would loosen the hydrant cap with a wrench causing several gallons of water to rush out, sending rapid streams down the gutters of the moderately inclined, one-way street. Her parents never allowed them to get close enough to the hydrant to get its full affect, but they were allowed to sit along the gutter, between parked cars, as the water surged around them.

This welcomed, instantly refreshing treat was always short-lived however. In a matter of ten minutes or less, the wailing sirens of fire engines could be heard in the distance. This only meant one thing, a disorganized evacuation. It's amazing how a hoard of people can disappear in seconds. Maybe it was because this practice was highly illegal.

The firemen would quickly recap the hydrant and be on their way. They knew, from experience, pursuing the culprits would have been a waste of time. For some reason, no one ever knew who did it—it was an unwritten urban code. Once the coast was clear, Annah would sit on her front stoop wrapped in a towel, feeling cooled and content.

...As the neighborhood deteriorated, my parents moved us to New Jersey. Talk about night and day! We went from being able to hear our neighbors argue to being exiled to a quaint little house on the prairie. The development we moved into consisted of no more than twenty homes spaced some distance apart, and the closest convenience store was three miles away, not down the street on the corner. It was the polar opposite of how I had lived for the first thirteen years of my life.

Any hoot, and back to the present, watching the neighborhood kids on their slip and slides and shooting hoops was a pleasant change to sitting in front of her computer. It was definitely a good idea that she got out and about.

Annah could see her house a block and a half away and it was a comforting sight. She had completed her first walk and was almost in the safety and comfort of home. As she walked up the driveway, she decided not to go inside right away. She wanted to be a part of civilization, to enjoy the engaging sounds and inspiriting sights that were playing all around her; to smell the subtle breath of the warm dry breeze; and to hear the children giggling while waiting in line for their cold treats from the ice cream novelty truck. There is nothing more symbolic of summer than the familiar tune blaring from the speakers of an ice cream truck.

Annah reflected on that morning's horoscope, which read, "Beginning a healthy regimen at this time is highly advisable. Exercise is important for building stamina and produces endorphins, which are essential in alleviating stress and creating a happier, healthier you. Be sure to include whole grains, fruit, vegetables and lean proteins in your diet. You will want to stay alert and active in the upcoming days."

…I've learned to accept the guidance the universe sends me through my horoscopes, so I'm off to the grocery store to stock up on healthy provisions. I need to supplement my protein bars with fruits, grains and maybe tuna fish. I'll slowly introduce these foods and hopefully get back to a balanced diet.

The store was virtually empty, which was a blessing for Annah. Even though she was brave enough to venture out and join the ranks of the living, she wasn't quite ready to engage in meaningless conversation with those chatty types, the ones who trick you into divulging the plights in your life, while filling you in on their latest gossip.

Annah wandered down the endless aisles of neatly stacked groceries, most of which had once occupied her shopping cart on a weekly visit. But on this shopping trip, she had no interest in sugary sweets, quenching flavored sodas, or frozen chicken nuggets. They were actually repulsive to her. She just followed the list she'd prepared and checked out as quickly as possible.

...I was able to carry the few bags I had into the house on one trip. But between running to the store and back, and putting the groceries away—I was worn out. I used my last ounce of energy to drag myself upstairs and fall across my bed. Before long, I was fast asleep.

Annah's blissful and regenerating midday nap was rudely interrupted by the sound of a diesel engine outside. It was around 3:30 when the daycare bus came to a halt a few houses down. As much as she longed to stay in bed, it was probably time for her to get up anyway and put something in her stomach. She opted for the peanut butter protein bar.

...I ripped the foil wrapper off at one end and took a small bite. All I can say is yuck! It tasted like an unsweetened glop of chocolate mixed with grains of sand, and raw boiled peanuts. I gagged down about one quarter of the bar and wrapped the rest for later. Hopefully, in time, I would crave and enjoy my old favorites—a medium-well steak, a buttery and lightly salted baked potato, and a garden salad. Right now though, such a heavy meal was making me nauseous just thinking about it.

The sun had finally gone down and the scorching afternoon heat transitioned into a comfortably warm night. Annah started out for her evening stroll, keeping a brisk but manageable pace. As she rounded the first corner, a growing fear of being followed was growing inside her. She looked over her shoulder several times, but there was no one in sight. She didn't necessarily hear footsteps, just an ill feeling that someone or something was lingering close by.

Rounding the second block, an inexplicable chill coursed down her spine. The corner lot, which was enclosed by a tall privacy fence, gave the eerie vibe that something was on the other side. Out of the corner of her eye, she thought she saw eyes peering through the gaps in the evenly spaced slats. She kept her steady pace and didn't react in fear or panic, but gave consideration to backtracking, fearing this thing may lunge out into her path at the end of the fence line.

So, just in case it wasn't matter of her imagination going wild, she began to recite a verse from the Bible that she had seen in a movie. It was Psalms 23:4, "...though

I walk through the valley of the shadow of death, I will fear no evil." That's the only part she remembered, so she repeated it several times, hoping to drive the point home that she wasn't afraid and had no intention of running from her fears.

With her sights set on the stop sign just yards away, Annah knew it was only a matter of turning the final corner before she was on the home stretch. And there it was, home sweet home. She walked up to the front porch and leaned over the rail, inhaling the refreshing night air while thanking the heavens she made it back safely. Everyone was housebound for the night, and now that Annah was out of harm's way, she decided she'd do the same.

She headed right for the shower and stood under the pulsating shower head for what seemed like forever. While the tiny beads massaged her head, she envisioned standing beneath a waterfall on a tropical island, reveling in the endless cascade of water, so peaceful and timeless. She pressed her hands against the wall of the shower, allowing the tepid water to rush down the curves of her body and dissolve her tensions. She stood motionless, savoring the moment.

Annah wrapped herself in an enormous towel, which had just been fluffed in the dryer. She looked like a geisha in a terry cloth kimono. After slipping into her PJ's and combing through her drenched and tangled strands of curly knots, she turned to the steamy mirror, wiping it with the back of her hand. As she leaned into the mirror, she noticed something very unsettling.

...When I looked in the mirror after my shower, I noticed a portion of my bangs were shorter on one side. They had been clipped to about an inch from my head. It wasn't just a couple of strands, it was an entire section. I guess I didn't notice it earlier because I wore a baseball cap all day. So, I had to wonder, who did this to me and why? I didn't see any clippings anywhere and I know my daughters wouldn't have done it. They had no reason to want to cut off my hair. If this was someone's idea of a joke, I can assure you, it was far from amusing. I guess the bigger question is why would someone do something so malicious?

Annah's mind was careening out of control with different scenarios inundating her mind. It was perplexing to her why anyone would want her hair. She reluctantly thought the only viable answer was that it was to be used for DNA testing. A while back Annah had read that you can obtain DNA from hair. So who wanted, or perhaps needed, her DNA?

A SIMULATING
EXPERIENCE

A nnah was clearly unnerved by the phantom butch-
ering of her hair. But she wasn't going to let it completely consume her, considering all the other bizarre incidents she had to decipher and deal with. She resolved
to go with the flow, hoping and praying that clarifying
explanations would be forthcoming.

She tuned the television to the comedy channel
believing a healthy dose of laughter would remedy her
malaise and promote a cheerier frame of mind. She may
have watched about ten minutes of a stand-up comic
struggling to wow the crowd, when she felt herself losing interest. Struggling to stay alert, she ultimately lost
the battle and dozed off.

Suffice it to say, travel was definitely on the night's
agenda. She came to rest in a foreign place, but very

different from the other realms she had already visited. Maneuvering fluidly along the streets of what appeared to be an Asian nation, she wasn't acknowledged by any one of the gazillion people humming along in this metropolis.

Closely resembling a more familiar New York City, it was chock full of fine restaurants, overstated billboards, couture shops, five star hotels and towering skyscrapers. The marquees that wrapped around the taller buildings flashed what appeared to be symbols in bright neon colors. Annah watched as the scrolling messages rounded the buildings looking for something familiar, maybe a word or two in English. But it was like deciphering hieroglyphics—nothing was remotely recognizable.

Annah moved buoyantly down the main thoroughfare in a blind search for clues of where she was. She had gone to the outskirts of the city where she happened upon a street sign which, to her relief, was written in English. It read, *Osaka University*, with an arrow pointing to the left. She followed the direction of the arrow and the subsequent arrows that followed. It brought her to the campus of a very modern, neo-eclectically designed school. The sign on the building indicated it was, *The School of Science and Engineering*.

In the center of the grand foyer was a round marble top table supported by vintage, brushed bronze legs. Laid out on the table were informational pamphlets, maps and an interesting display for a macromolecular symposium to be hosted by the school that upcoming February. Annah was not familiar with macromolecular science, so she grabbed a brochure and quickly scanned through it. Still not sure of this particular area of science, she concluded that it had something to do with physics or biology. She also grabbed a campus map, and the handout about the history of the university.

"Established in 1931, this was Japan's 6th imperial university. As a result of a governmental reform program, the university grew to include five faculties: Science; Medicine; Engineering; Letters; and Law, and eventually graduate schools and research institutes were established. The School of Engineering Science was the first of its kind in Japan because it incorporated both Science and Engineering disciplines."

Annah now knew she was in Japan.

She peered down the length of the tiled hallway, which donned the appearance of a typical office floor plan in a professional building; windows, nameplates and heavy wooden doors, each with a secure keypad entry. She started down the corridor, stopping at the many observation windows, hoping to catch a glimpse of what was inside. The slatted blinds were drawn in most of them, so she couldn't see much, but assumed they were offices, classrooms, or possibly laboratories.

At the far end of the hallway, a door was ajar and the blinds were open. She hurried down and peered through the window, hopefully to pick up on anything that would explain, or make sense of why the heck she was brought there. The room was amply lit by overhead fluorescent lights, and judging by the furnishings in the room, it appeared to be a robotics laboratory.

In the center of the room, was a large structure assembled on a rolling cart. At first glance it looked like crumpled aluminum foil molded into the shape of a creature, with metal flex tubes for limbs, a plastic tube attached to what looked like a ventilator, and color-coded wires fused to a metal sheet, like a circuit board; the wires were connected to an elaborate computer system on a shelf beneath the cart. Annah followed the trail of one of the wires, the yellow one to be exact; it was routed to a device similar to a heart monitor. A steady stream of thermal paper was flowing from the bottom of the monitor with four different waveforms printing in continuous lines.

*July 30*th

I went into the room to get a closer look. Nothing was labeled and there were no research papers or files lying on the desk. To the left was an adjoining room, possibly an office. I flipped on the switch just inside the door and as the light came on, I saw a human-like figure sitting in the corner of the room. I was startled, then horrified. It was a life-like replica—OF ME! I was trembling as I got closer.

Annah called out as she approached, "Hello?"

There was no response, to which she wasn't at all disappointed. She doesn't know what she would have done if it had answered. Its fixed stare was cold and intensely grim. Once she was assured it wouldn't cause her any harm, she inched closer. Her stealthy footsteps were very calculated—had this thing so much as twitched, she was ready to make a fleeting exit.

Staring herself in the face, and not being in front of a mirror, was probably the creepiest feeling she'd ever experienced. She made several distinct facial movements, directly in its face, to make sure it wasn't just an elaborate illusion, but its face remained still with a solid blank expression. Then she ran her hands over the clone's clothes and hair, withdrawing quickly when her fingers got entangled in its synthetic locks, accidently pulling out a loose fitting, metal fanned hair clip.

...I reached forward towards its face. With my fingers stretched out, I brushed along the side of its cheek. I was blown away by how soft and subtle the skin felt. The eyebrows, nose, cheek bones and lips were all mirror images of my facial features. Its hair, although styled differently, was an exact match to my color and texture. Was this why my hair was snipped? Did they need a hair swatch to fabricate this thing's hair? The body itself was nothing more than a plastic mannequin, but I'm sure its human-like parts would be added later.

Annah believed she had been cloned in the form of an android, but didn't know why and, unfortunately, there wasn't anyone around to ask. She went back out to the main laboratory to mentally collect as much information as she could. She walked around the foiled object several times and concluded that all the tubes and wires would eventually be the components of the android's internal makeup; the components that would eventually bring this thing to life—its heartbeat, movements and expressions.

Annah couldn't understand what was going on. Was this replica created to eventually replace her? She knew it would never be able to fool her family and friends. She also realized she sounded ridiculous, but in the absence of any other explanation, what was she to think.

Doctor Oliver, as usual was calm yet eager to hear what she had to tell him. Annah had decided to focus only on the clone thing. She didn't want to confuse the doctor or muddle his mind with all the other stuff. When she got done with her story and her suspicions, he leaned forward in his chair.

She waited patiently. He started, "Annah, as we have discussed, you can't leap to any conclusions and you can't rule out that these astral trips are merely dreams. Important and revealing dreams, true, but none the less dreams."

She reached in her pocket and retrieved the metal hair clip, placing it on the desk before him. Both gazed at it. He felt there was nothing unusual about it—a common women's hair item. His eyes asked, "So?"

She said, "This isn't mine. *I've never seen it before, before last night that is.*"

"Are you sure?"

"Very. Look at it. I guarantee you won't find one like it in any store in this area. Now I don't expect you to go looking for it, just believe me when I tell you, it's not a familiar item in this culture."

He continued to gaze at her.

"My clone was wearing this in her hair. As you can see my hair is too short and thin to use this type of clip."

After an awkward pause he asked, "So where did it come from?

"This morning, I found it dangling from one of the buttons on my nightshirt. It had come loose when I ran my fingers through the clone's hair."

Doctor Oliver cocked his head. "This is possibly the same kind of evidence as found at other supernatural events, so while that doesn't necessarily prove anything it is evidence that you have traveled beyond the parameters of your natural world."

"So, you're saying I actually..."

"No, I'm not saying that for sure. I'm simply saying it is possible. That's where you should leave it. As long as these astral trips don't harm you, and as long as you seem to gain knowledge and insight from them, I'd leave it at that until and unless something else happens that definitely verifies it."

...The doctor, as usual, was so realistic and rational that he helped me to believe that these things were not simply my imagination gone wild, but had real meaning and real significance. Maybe I am a link to the other side. I've heard some people are. In any case, I felt better knowing that the good doctor wasn't writing any of this off to an overly active and wandering mind.

Annah was awakened by a knock at the front door. She slid out of bed and walked over to the upstairs window. Parked in front of her house was an Express Delivery truck. She quickly ran downstairs to sign for the package then went back upstairs to lie down for a little while longer.

THE KEY

After Annah ordered her reading, she began to receive email solicitations offering such magical items as ensorcelled amulets, runic rhymes, and relics, supposedly found in sacred archaeological digs; and to validate these claims, each object came with a certificate of authenticity. After a while, Annah began to skip the tedious task of reading through the cleverly composed promises, implausible overtures, and testimonials of the fame and fortune these enchanted items notoriously guaranteed. Other than being mentally provocative reads, she found they usually held no merit.

One particular email, however, grabbed her attention with its opening statement, "I have the key that will unlock the doors to the buried secrets that rightfully belong to you. All your current worries will disappear, and you will experience the happiness you so desperately want and need." This one just seemed more personal than generic, like it was intended solely for her. It proposed the purchase of a mystical key, and an instructional booklet with spells, chants and rituals, to bring the key's magical power to life.

She filled out the form and ordered her magical key for nineteen dollars and ninety-nine cents.

July 31st

A few weeks ago, I received an email offer that called out to me. It was probably just another gimmick like the others, but to me it seemed more personal. There was something unique about it and I knew I needed to have it. I wasn't so much intrigued by what it promised, but more for what it represented. It was a key. It may have just been an instinctual hunch, but I felt it had a symbolic meaning, like a legend key, to enable me to decipher the random bits of information I've accumulated, and continue to acquire, from my travels.

Annah opened the Express Delivery shipping bag and pulled out a small brown box; neither the box nor the bag had anything printed on it identifying the sender, so she wasn't sure what was inside. She stared at this mystery box for a couple of seconds, testing her intuitive powers to try to guess what it could be. But after straining her brain, with no results, she resorted to slitting the packaging tape open with a steak knife. She rummaged through a thick layer of crumbled brown paper and several small foam peanuts before exposing a small key in a slender, lock-top plastic bag. She reached in and pulled out the bag, along with a booklet that was buried beneath it.

Measuring about three inches, it wasn't shaped like the type of key we use today; it was more distinctive of a vintage jewelry box key, tarnished bronze with a marbling of gunmetal. The stem, or hollow tube that is inserted into a lock, had a notched tooth-like bit at one end and the bow handle, on the other end, boasted an ornate design, similar to the Celtic cross, with welded beading at the junctures.

The booklet, a cheap paperback with an unadorned cover, displayed its title in a standard courier font, "The Key: Unlock Its Mystical Power." It modestly included only thirty or so sparsely printed pages; the first being an introduction, and cursory instruction on how to unleash the key's power. The remaining pages included rhythmical verses, spells, rituals, and incantations. Annah fanned through the pages with her thumb, randomly stopping at one of the spells. She recited it as if she were a wizard casting a spell.

This key in which you firmly hold,
Will bring you money,
One-hundred fold.
It's yours for the taking but please beware,
You must slay the beast,
If you dare!
The keeper frowns on those who wait,
So hasten your pace
And open the gate.

A very powerful surge coursed through her body, and beads of perspiration formed on her forehead; a murky mist of buyer's remorse surrounded her. The key, along with its magical spells, were very powerful and possessed a supernatural, ungodly quality. By reading this spell aloud, she couldn't help but to think she'd initiated something she might end up regretting later, like she'd opened Pandora's Box, releasing evil spirits and demons that had been locked away for centuries.

Annah looked down at her hand. She had gripped the key so firmly her fingernails imprinted her palm. As much as she tried, she couldn't loosen her grip, so she frantically grabbed each finger with her other hand, prying them open until finally the key popped out and onto the floor.

Annah admitted it wasn't one of her more brilliant ideas, delving right into all of this hocus-pocus and witchery without knowing anything about it. Even though it may have been too late, she opened the booklet to the first page and began reading. The first few pages basically reiterated the phraseology from the initial offer, followed by a page containing two simple, intriguing statements centered on the page, "This key will unlock a world of treasures for you. Just learn how to use its power and you will want for nothing."

The first chapter established the instructions, or methods, on how to attract spirits into your life. It didn't say good or evil, just spirits. But after the first handful of pages, she noticed the overall inflection began to change. It began to take on a more hostile tone, with maleficent undercurrents. The closing sentence was the most disconcerting, "To attract these forces into your life, you must begin by dispelling any preconceived beliefs. You must begin with a clean slate if you want to entertain the infinite powers of this otherworldly mysticism."

It felt dark and chilling, definitely not the comforting vibe of amiable forces. She leafed through the remainder of the pages, stopping to read partial passages here and there. The images of what she had read didn't paint a pleasant picture. She envisioned the devastation that could erupt if these powers were unharnessed, questioning if it had the potential to wreak havoc on a universal level.

Annah knew she needed to dispose of this black magic paraphernalia as soon as possible. She replaced the key and booklet in the box and groped through the junk drawer for tape to seal it shut. She thought she had successfully encased the evil, but some of its residual effects lingered. The lights began to flicker in their high hat fixtures, like SOS distress signals from a ship; trying to convey an important message or warning. The tingling vibrations, once again, pulsed through her body, a clear sign that this act angered the entity.

Hurriedly, she brought the box outside to the garbage can and buried it under a few layers of already decaying trash. She couldn't risk it falling into the wrong hands. Hopefully, she'd disposed of these materials before she awakened or summoned some evil creature or dark beast.

Annah was struggling with an inability to know the difference between the truth and deception. She put on a kettle of water for tea—ginger and orange herbal, to help settle her nerves. While the tea was brewing, she reflected on her travel to Osaka University and what she had observed there, namely the android that was created to look like her.

After she finished the last drop of her soothing comfort, she decided to venture out of the house. Hopefully getting out and about would shake her melancholic state. Driving through her neighborhood somberly reminded her of the lonely existence she had been living the past few weeks, so she ventured out to the market to pick up some toiletries.

After loading her hand basket with soap, deodorant, disposable shavers, and other necessities, she leisurely walked down every aisle of the store to make sure she didn't need other things that may have slipped her mind. On her way to the checkout, she stopped at the magazine kiosk where she scanned the array of titles, ranging alphabetically from 'Additions and Decks' to 'Weekend Getaways'. Two particular magazines caught her eye with their featured articles, so in the basket they went, along with a crossword and variety puzzle book.

On her drive home, with her windows down and favorite CD playing, Annah took note of how calm and content she felt. She knew it would only benefit her recovery to get out of the house more. The light bulb finally went on in her head, illuminating the fact that her home had become her safe refuge and it was isolating her from the rest of the world. It felt good to be around people, even though she still didn't feel comfortable engaging in conversation just yet. She was also very excited about her unplanned, mind stimulating purchases and decided to not bottle herself up inside, but to read outside until it got too dark to see.

Annah positioned the chaise lounge in the upright position on the back patio. With magazines in one hand and cold lemonade in the other, she was off to the races. It had been a while since she so selfishly indulged herself. And yes, sadly, this was a form of indulgence.

One of the magazines was titled, "Scientific Mind." Her attraction to this particular magazine was the featured article, "The Science of Burnout – Why it happens and how to stop it." She thought if she learned more about brain overload or burnout in general, she might be able to translate it to what was going on with her, or learn more about what brings a person to that point, or most importantly, how to recover from this type of trauma.

The article was very informative and pretty much confirmed everything she had already read. Annah earmarked the page and went inside to refill her glass, and grab a pillow to support her back. When she came back out, the magazine was opened to different page. Apparently the wind flipped it a few pages forward, to an article entitled, "Future Shock: A Date with a Robot."

It was about a computer scientist, Hiroshi Ishiguro, who had done his research at Osaka University. His claim to fame was a life-like android he modeled after a local celebrity. The journalist who conducted the interview was overwhelmed by the human qualities the robot possessed, and continued on to commend Ishiguro's extraordinary accomplishment.

Annah realized this was not some weird coincidence. Something very bizarre was going on. Now more than ever, she knew the importance of piecing together all the information from her astral travels; it was the only way she would come close to a reasonable explanation.

...It had crossed my mind to blog my story, or to find a confidant that wouldn't think I was totally bananas. But quite frankly, I wasn't sold on the fact that I wasn't bonkers. It was a preposterous story—even I'm having trouble coming to terms with it all. My other concern with sharing this story—there was a distinct possibility of disclosing century old secrets to the enemy, that secret underworld conspiracy group.

KING SOLOMON

That damned key, whose ambiguity continued to haunt Annah, had her wondering what she would have learned if she had held onto it just a little while longer or studied it more closely before tossing it away so hastily. Perhaps it wasn't the wisest decision she'd ever made, sending it to a trash dump where it could eventually be found. But even though she no longer had it in her possession, she couldn't help but feel an obligation to find out why it surfaced in the first place, and how she ended up with it.

*August 1*st

I knew I wouldn't be able to let it go until I either knew this key wasn't just another gimmick, or if I was to figure out some underlying meaning. Doing an image search of the key, there were dozens that shared its basic characteristics. I enlarged one of the images that seemed like a relatively close match and studied it for quite a while.

The shape and color bore a striking resemblance, although one-quarter its size, to the key illustrated in the historical accounts of when Ben Franklin discovered electricity. The idea of electricity ignited another far-reaching concept in Annah. She correlated the vibrations she had felt at night to the type of surge you would feel from an electrical current. Taken in that context, it made perfect sense. What she couldn't bring meaning to, however, was the spell book that accompanied the key.

So Annah dismissed that theory and decided to read-dress the notion of it symbolizing a legend key, perhaps a map interpretation. She grabbed a few sheets of paper and began to draw a map, using the locations of her astral travels as landmarks, and the morsels of minutiae from each location as the legend, then plotted them on the map. She stared at her amateurish attempt to create something meaningful, and in the midst of trying to make sense of it, realized it was a mixed bag of nothing—she had hit another dead end.

But she wasn't ready to put it to rest. In fact, because her obsessive desire to figure this out was even more stimulated, she once again consulted with the omnipotent source of infinite answers—the internet. It was the only resource that was readily available that could assist her in unraveling this convoluted ball of wax. She typed the string, "famous keys," which returned pages of links, most of which were irrelevant. She didn't want to invest too much time looking for that proverbial needle in a haystack, so she needed to be more specific with her search criteria.

Annah combed through her journal for significant words and phrases that would narrow the results exponentially. She started grouping words together, beginning with her first travel to Greece. She tried oracle keys, Athena keys, wisdom keys, Greek keys, and even Athena and mystical keys. Nothing legitimate came back, so she went on to search Eye of Horus and keys, pyramid keys and even went as far as searching android keys—still nothing!

After searching for hours, with nothing to show for it, she became frustrated and discouraged as she neared the end of her investigative rope. Reaching forward to close her laptop, she noticed, out of the corner of her eye, an advertisement posted by a notable bookseller. They were announcing the debut of, what they believed to be, the next bestseller. The cover of the book was captivating; beautifully illustrated and titled with gold embossed lettering, "Solomon's Key."

It was one of those moments when you look up to the heavens and acknowledge their intervention with a softly whispered, "Thank You." She typed the phrase, *Solomon's Key*, into the search engine. Numerous results were listed, and seemed to go on forever. Forgetting the fact that she was tired, and on the brink of shutting down for the day, pure adrenaline kept her going. She immediately poured her restored energy into this endeavor, clicking on each link, reading every word. She wasn't so much looking for a reputable source as she was in finding something that would validate the importance of the key. And at that moment, as if her thoughts were being read by the great beyond, the answer she was look-ing for displayed on the screen.

"...although not a key that unlocked a secret cham-ber in Solomon's temple, it was instead a voluminous tome of secrets, formulas, codes and encryptions. This book contained a collection of pentacle shaped symbols, conjurations and curses; and most importantly encoded epistles from the Gods detailing all of creation. King Solomon, of Israel, had written this manuscript in an unconventional, unprecedented, cryptic code so only his son, Rehoboam, or those that were bequeathed the hono-rarium of wisdom by the Mother Goddess herself, could interpret its meaning and powers. Upon Rehoboam's death, the manuscript disappeared and was rumored to have been entombed with his body.

"Thousands of years later, the tomb was discovered and excavated by archaeologists. The time-worn manu-script was found with pages seared—some completely dematerialized and evaporated with the introduction of the unstable atmosphere. In an effort to preserve the surviving fragments, they were quickly moved to a con-trolled storage facility where masterful cryptologists were called upon to begin the wearisome task of deciphering the fragmented, heterodox code.

"Several attempts were made to decrypt the hiero-glyphics and archaic scrawls but experts agreed that it lacked a consistent standard compared to other writings representative of that period. It was then concluded, based on the beliefs of this civilization, that it was only decipherable by a chosen few, a canonist perhaps."

Flashbacks to the paperback and key Annah had discarded had her feeble mind employing the notion that the universe, with its perverse sense of humor, had endowed her with the sacred writings of the King himself. She didn't know whether to celebrate the honor of being 'the chosen one' or to damn the universe for implicating her in the first place. Thinking back to the day she received the package, she now believed the evil entities were waiting in the wings, haunting vigilantly in the shadows for her to read those coveted secrets aloud; waiting for her to inadvertently disclose all that had been so carefully concealed and protected for several millennia.

...My appetite to learn more still wasn't fully satisfied. With many questions, especially about King Solomon's secrets and the power he possessed, I have become consumed by this quest that is slowly and completely devouring my life. But I know I won't be able to return to a normal state of mind until I quench this thirst. I have every intention of ploughing through the uncertain terrain ahead of me, at all costs.

For several minutes Annah sat still trying to silence her internal dialogue and compartmentalize her thoughts that had become a stockpile of mental disorganization. She needed to clear the clutter and download her thoughts into a meaningful, well organized document, establishing a time line with detailed notes. Stretching her fingers while correcting her posture, as if she was about to play a piece on the ebony and ivory, she opened a new document in a word processing application and began transferring her mental dossier into a tidy list that she could quickly and easily refer back to.

Once the list was composed, she read each item one by one, over and over again trying to establish a cohesive theme. Nothing was meshing together, which only confused her more. She remembered The Contract advising her to not worry about her immediate future—that the planets would show her the right way to go.

…My mind was in desperate need of a well-deserved break. I felt it would be refreshing to engage in some form of physical activity to get those endorphins stimulated. Besides, blankly staring at the computer screen wasn't getting me any closer to my objective. The skies were looking a little sinister, so outdoor activities were definitely out of the question. And even though my house was seen by others as the epitome of tidiness, I felt a quick once over would satisfy my need to have everything in order. It was metaphorical in a sense; if my house was orderly and clean, my mind would also be uncluttered and run at peak efficiency. Once I got started, there was no stopping me until every room was clean and sterile.

After Annah finished up, she decided to perform a spiritual cleansing of the house. She verbalized her desire for the evil spirits to leave and give her peace and serenity in her personal space. Just the act itself made her hopeful that the mischievous antics would end, and joy and happiness would be restored.

She lit her favorite cinnamon and spice candle and placed it on the kitchen counter, and put on a kettle to brew some well-deserved chai spiced tea. As she sipped on the perfect blend of black tea, clove and nutmeg, she reflected on the challenges in her life, specifically when she'd be returning to work. She feared if she didn't go back soon, she wouldn't have a job to go back to. Just thinking about it was mentally draining. It was time for her midday siesta.

It was almost two in the afternoon when Annah sprawled across her freshly washed and neatly tucked bedding; she drifted off almost immediately. Her pillow top mattress soon became a feathery white cloud that floated aimlessly through the heavens. Visions of a blissful future manifested before her eyes, and she felt a profound sense of optimism and contentedness.

But, Annah's bliss evaporated into the afternoon sky as she slowly descended towards mother earth, towards an unfamiliar landscape that grew larger the further she fell. She maneuvered between mountain peaks that varied in height and distinction with rivers flowing through their valleys. She landed in front of an enormous concrete commune that sat atop a massive plateau.

Enveloped in the limestone-flanked fortress was a compound. There were many different buildings, each with its own unique design and each, more than likely, serving a significant purpose. One of the buildings, the most exquisite and grandiose, resembled a lavishly embellished version of the Lincoln Memorial, with its Greek Doric architecture. Annah could only imagine it to have been the hub of this antiquated community, a religious temple, if she had to guess. She knew her time there had to be totally devoted to exploring every intricate detail.

Annah entered through the main entrance, and continued on through the open-air atrium that was bedecked with a white, stone tiled floor. The purity of the walkway gave an overall sense of sanctity. She slowly gravitated towards the semi-circular stairs leading up to the temple, where she was met by two very sturdy, ornately carved, marble columns. They were poised vigilantly like royal guardsmen to protect the hallowed building from unwelcomed guests. The majestic gold-plated doors opened slowly and Annah was ushered in by a gentle current. The grandeur of her entrance was like that of an exclusive, invitation-only ball, except no one greeted her at the door, nor was her arrival announced.

Once inside, the doors slowly came together. Annah was in a room that was a lusterless, more modest area—perhaps the foyer. She walked down the center aisle through the worship area, and past the pulpit to a private sanctuary. There were five steps that led to another door. This one didn't magically open as she approached, in fact, it was locked.

...I couldn't imagine why that particular door was locked, but it made me that much more eager to find a way in. Searching through drawers and cubbies, I found nothing that resembled a key. Just behind the altar was a thick tapestry hanging from the ceiling, like Grandma's old insulated draperies. I slowly drew the heavy curtain to one side; it revealed five hidden doors. Methodically, I pushed them open, one at a time. They all served a particular purpose. One was a meeting room, two others were used for the storage of sacred objects, and one was a prayer room or confessional. The fifth door opened to an unlit hallway.

Curiosity motivated Annah to enter the corridor of darkness. She passed her hand lightly along the crumbling stone walls, as a guide, brushing against metal sconces, with petrified wax dangling from their arms. She was only a few steps away from a second door when a furious force pressed against her body, holding her at bay with its intense power. She pressed on with every bit of strength she had, but struggling and fighting was no match for the invisible wall. Whatever was in the hallway with her would not allow her to enter the secret room. It was either warning her that she was about to tread on very dangerous ground, or whatever was in the room was strictly forbidden. For the first time in all her astral travels, she genuinely felt threatened to the point of retreating. She reluctantly backed off, as did the powerful energy. As she scurried to the front doors of the temple, she was convinced she had stumbled upon something so coveted, it was heavily guarded.

Annah returned to her physical body, still frightened and trembling from the dark force that stopped her in that dark hallway of the temple. She feared her journey was now treading through murky waters, burdening her with truths that would sink her to the bottom of an angry sea. Her only consolation, and driving force to continue, was in knowing that her courage and perseverance were being smiled upon by the stars.

She remembered The Contract stating that a vital opportunity would be offered to her. At first it didn't make much sense, but now she was willing to believe anything was possible. Knowing it seemed preposterous and totally inconceivable in the right frame of mind, she deemed her latest theory totally credible in her current altered mindset.

Annah believed, because she was the chosen recipient of the King's manuscript, that she was being groomed for a dignified role—that of a goddess. Some higher power had secretly been observing her, since her birth, watching as she learned and absorbed the ways of humanity, waiting for her to awaken and assume this prestigious role. Now polished and prepared, she was ready to transition to her intended divine status.

...All my life I had dreamed that one day I would be someone special, someone people admired and looked up to, and ultimately wanted to be like—a role model. Butterflies filled my stomach just knowing I may soon be that person. I have so much to give, and want to make so many things right in this world. I just hope my hunches are right and this is the opportunity The Contract is talking about. I still want to do a little more research though, so after my ophthalmologist appointment this morning (turns out I have a condition called, chronic dry eye), I'll go to the public library to read more about the late King Solomon. The internet is an excellent resource, but I want to get out and be around people. So I'm going to get my information the old-fashioned way—through books.

It had been years since Annah stepped foot in a library and so many things had changed. She looked for a card catalog, only to find out it was now computerized. It was good to see that the modest, hometown library joined the technology of the twenty-first century. She took a seat in front of the only available monitor and, after typing a few keywords, was able to locate an entire shelf dedicated to the late King Solomon. She randomly pulled a few of the books from their sequentially filed spots and staked her claim to an unoccupied table.

Annah laid the books out in a row in front of her in hopes to learn more about the King, his temple, and all the related legends and myths from his time. She began with the one that adorned an illustration of Solomon's temple on the cover. With a few sheets of paper she pulled from the libraries' recycle bin, and a yellow stubby pencil she borrowed from the reference desk, she was armed and ready to consume as much information as possible.

She began reading, "The temple, built by the late King Solomon, was located in the city of Jerusalem. Solomon, who was believed to have been born in 1011 BC, was the son of King David, known as the wisest of all men."

Annah paused to digest what she had just read. Goose bumps dimpled her arms, and a cold shiver chilled her body. The number sequence '1011' leapt off the page. That was the same number pattern that had become prominent in her life. She was in awe that it finally took on meaning, implicitly verifying that she was exactly where she was supposed to be, learning exactly what she was supposed to learn. However, the thought of it all being a coincidence lingered about in the back of her mind.

She read on, "Rulers from all over the world would travel long distances just to kneel before David, to hear his words of wisdom. When Solomon became king, after the death of his father, he built a temple in his honor. King David had always aspired to build a temple on the mount, but this ambitious endeavor was never fulfilled. The temple was lavishly constructed with gold overlays, marble columns at its entrance, and the finest stone floors. It housed many sacred objects, including the Ark of the Covenant, and the many buildings inside the confines were said to have accommodated royalty.

"Many proverbs, including Proverbs 24:14-22, were written by King Solomon. This particular proverb emphasized that we must live a virtuous life, without becoming envious of evildoers or those that seem to have had their desires fulfilled by living an avaricious, self-serving existence. All his writings were inspired by his wisdom, a trait inherently passed down by his father.

"That being said, King Solomon should have heeded his own words. He became materialistic, corrupt and perverted. He began to protect his wealth by hiding his possessions in secret chambers throughout the compound. He felt his writings would be taken from him and decided to lock them away in undisclosed locations. Eventually, his self-indulgence caused the fall of his kingdom, and years later, the fall of his temple. He paid the ultimate price for turning his back on the universe that had blessed him with wisdom, wealth and power."

...I feel this exact scenario is playing out in these modern times. The wealthier and more powerful seem to have neglected those who aren't as fortunate and make no qualms in flaunting the fact they are well above them. If history does repeat itself, their greed and ignorance will seal their unfortunate fate.

"During his reign, King Solomon came to adore a goddess by the name of Sophia, Goddess of Wisdom, noted for her intuitive intelligence and regarded as the wise bride of Solomon by the Jewish people. They developed a deep and profound relationship, and because of his devout reverence for her, he erected a statue in her honor.

"Sophia became a universal figure, highly regarded and recognized in many cultures, but referred to by different names. In Egypt, for instance, she was sometimes referred to as Isis. Some theologians believe that Mary Magdalene was Sophia incarnate; and others believe she was symbolized by the dove that descended from the heavens—which is known in the Christian faith as the Holy Spirit."

…Bible school sure didn't teach me that. What if the Holy Spirit really is Goddess Sophia? That adds another layer to this complex puzzle. I was anxious to read more about Sophia, especially who she was and if this myth was true. I logged back in to the library's computer catalog to find books on the wisdom goddess.

WROCLAW

August 2nd

As a morning ritual I checked my email, just in case a certain someone finally came to his senses and decided to beg for my forgiveness. I didn't get one from Lance, but I did get one from another certain someone. After deleting all the spam mail and advertisements, a single email sat alone, in the unopened status. It was an email from my supervisor. He was requesting that I visit work to discuss my outstanding workload and to return my company issued laptop.

Annah's stomach lurched convulsively. She recalled explaining in her last email that she had an illness and would be out on disability. Was he planning to fire her? Why else would he want her to come in? She couldn't deal with this, not in her current condition. Unable to go into work and risk being stared at, judged or ridiculed, she burst into tears just thinking what a jerk he was. His lack of compassion only confirmed his detached and insensitive nature. She confesses that initially she hadn't gone into specifics about why she was out, but she felt then, and more so now, that she shouldn't have had to. It was personal and she had already offered sufficient information. Besides, she was legitimately out on disability and that alone should have prompted him to let her be. He obviously wasn't grasping the delicate nature of her disorder.

After releasing all her anger and frustration through tears, and reining in her irritation, she managed to compose a civil response. Not that he deserved one, she just felt obligated. She merely offered to send the laptop in with a friend, and that a visit to the workplace wouldn't be possible at that time. Knowing he wasn't going to take that very well, and dreading his response, she shut down her computer to delay the inevitable and burrowed in the sofa.

Annah repositioned herself several times agonizing over the fact her email probably pissed him off. He was most likely under the gun with deadlines, and because he didn't know programming or what she did on a daily basis for that matter, he was in a very compromising position. Her work cases were undoubtedly backing up, putting even more pressure on him. He was getting unwanted attention from the higher ups, so sooner or later he would have to admit his inadequacies.

Realistically, Annah knew she couldn't put off the inevitable by ignoring the issue, so she logged back on to her laptop. There were no new emails in her inbox, specifically the dreaded response, which was unusual. She refreshed her computer screen to force the pages to reload and update, but instead of a slew of new emails displaying, a message popped up that she wasn't connected to the internet.

...!@#$%^&, pretty much sums up what I shouted out. I love my computer when it works, but hate it when it decides not to love me back. Thank goodness I am computer literate or else my computer and all related devices would have been tossed in the garbage. I refused to let this hiccup get the better of me, so I followed protocol I learned while serving time on the help desk. The first line of fire was to unplug the modem, wait, and plug it back in. Still, there was no connection. I even tried my favorite remedy and cursed at the screen a couple of times. Surprisingly it didn't work, but the swearing did help me feel a little better. As a last resort, I clicked on network connections. Sure enough, my network wasn't listed as one of those available. There were four listed, three being my neighbors and the fourth was that mysterious network named, Wroclaw. Who did this network belong to? Was someone sitting outside the house, in a surveillance van accessing my computer remotely? It was time to take it off the back burner and deal with it once and for all.

Annah listlessly stared at the computer screen feeling anchored by all the disconnected pieces of information she had gathered so far. She needed to find the association between the overseas travel, the cave, the android and now, Wroclaw. Not giving up hope that it would all be revealed in due time, she couldn't help but fear her road to discovery was beginning to develop potholes, obstacles and forks.

She carefully considered all she had done so far and reviewed her objectives one more time. All in all, truth be told, how else would she occupy her days. At least this scavenger hunt was keeping her mind active and believe it or not, she felt she was getting better with each passing day. Besides, if she didn't continue, she would never get the answers she was looking for and would always wonder, "What if?"

Annah restarted her computer and finally her network was listed. Now that she was connected to the internet, her first order of business was to find out if Wroclaw was a person, place, or thing, and if it should be included as a noteworthy part of her journey. The search results that came back overwhelmingly established that Wroclaw was indeed a place.

"Located in Poland, Wroclaw is the fourth largest city behind Warszawa, Lodz and Krakow. Actually over the years, it was a part of Bohemia, Austria, Germany, Prussia and Poland. It wasn't until 1945, because of the border changes after World War II, that is was officially declared a part of Poland."

Other than these somewhat boring facts, nothing popped out as being relevant to piecing the puzzle together. She decided to change her search to list landmarks, notable people and historical facts. These results were at least a little more interesting. It turns out, the most prominent landmark, and crowning glory of Wroclaw, is its university, Wroclaw University.

She clicked on the link for the University's web site. It appeared to have quite an impressive genetic research department. Its banner page read, "The first and foremost focus of The University of Wrocław is scientific research. Our continued success has been recognized internationally, increasing our funding by 80% compared to previous years."

Somewhere in the middle of reading, Annah dozed off. She traveled back a few centuries, possibly to the nineteenth, to a small renaissance town. The narrow cobblestone streets and brightly burning gaslights helped define this dated era. The buildings that flanked the cobbled streets were structurally unique, as well as vibrant and colorful. The architectural styles followed no specific pattern; one was painted royal blue, and tapered to a point from the third floor to the attic; another was a bright pink five story colonial while its attached neighbor, boasted a lime green color that replicated that of a grand 'haus' in Germany.

...There was no activity, which lead me to believe I had arrived in the wee hours of the morning and the entire town was asleep. The street level shops, which most likely bustled during the day, were dark and deserted, with their shutters latched and doors locked. It was like a ghost town, eerie, empty, and fully inspirited. I found myself looking over my shoulder every few seconds fearing a villain like Jack the Ripper was on the prowl; waiting in the wings to lunge from a dark alleyway for the opportune moment to mutilate the only living soul on the street—with no one around to hear the blood-curdling screams.

While peering down what appeared to be the main artery of town, a narrowing road with no end in sight, a dense white fog rose out of nowhere. It totally obscured her vision as it rolled towards her. She couldn't see past it and she couldn't escape it, her only option was to walk into it using the cobblestones beneath her feet as navigational tools.

The heavy mist eventually dissipated, to where she could see a glimmering light just ahead. It looked like the moon hidden behind a cluster of clouds, shining brightly, with a hazy aura. A glint of light flashed in the corner of her eye, so she turned in its direction. It was a deflection from a metal pole. Affixed to the top was a slate plaque that read, *Odra River*.

It was mounted at the foot of an arched bridge, barely the width of a car, with cracked and worn mortar slabs on both sides for foot traffic. The handrails, as well as the side guard rails, were beautifully crafted; tinged ever so slightly with the green hue of oxidized copper. This was a masterpiece that only highly skilled ironworkers could have constructed.

Directly in the middle of the span, the metalwork arched high across the width in a crisscross pattern. Annah was mesmerized by its charm, along with the breathtaking view of the mirror of lights dancing over the small ripples of the river. There was only one word worthy of describing this animated portrait—Magnifique!

Just on the other side of the bridge stood one of the most spectacular buildings she had ever seen. It occupied roughly five city blocks and boasted an authoritative demeanor. Far from being a connoisseur of world travel, and relying solely on photographs, it bore a striking resemblance to the monarchial stronghold, Buckingham Palace.

Candles were burning in the countless windows of the four-story, Headington stone building. Annah walked up to the street-level entrance, at the center point. She read the sign that was mounted to the stone, *Uniwersytet Wroclawski.*

...As I was walking towards this massive structure, I experienced a déjà vu moment. This was the very building I had researched earlier this morning. It was Wroclaw University. Now it was time to find out why I was brought here and why Wroclaw is so important to the grand scheme of things.

Annah stepped inside the portal, to a foyer that was just as overwhelmingly beautiful as the outer façade. The ceilings were domed with stained glass skylights at the peak; richly marbled pillars lined the numerous ten-foot doorways; and intricate stone-carved details embellished the walls. Above one of the doors was a marble sculpture of woman with a toga draped over one shoulder, and a shield resting by her arm. It reminded her of Goddess Athena.

She wandered down one of the corridors, taking in all the sculpted busts sitting motionless in shadow-boxes; renaissance inspired artwork and paintings seemingly restored, but clearly replicas and colorful pottery placed strategically to fill voids in the bare white walls. She peeked into the many rooms as she ambled down the hallway. As she neared the end, she could hear voices. She stopped at the doorway and peered into the room. Everyone silenced their chatter as she entered, and directed their attention to Annah.

"Welcome, we've been waiting for you." A man slowly emerged from the small crowd.

"Why am I here?" Annah couldn't imagine what he meant by that.

Without acknowledging that she had posed a question, they quickly escorted her to an adjoining room. There were scientists wearing traditional white lab coats: microscopes, computers and test tubes covered the green laminate counters and goggles and latex gloves were scattered among the apparatus. They isolated Annah to the corner of the room and carried on, business as usual, exchanging dialogue in their heavily accented dialect that she struggled to understand. It was as if she had become invisible.

...I listened intently in an effort to gain some insight as to what they were conversing about and hopefully why I was there. I saw several vials, some empty and some filled with samplings of blood. The filled vials had labels centered on them. My name, as well as the name of the testing lab I had gone to for blood work, was printed on the labels. I know this is all a part of a conspiracy that everyone is in on except me. At this point, I'm not sure if I'm more curious or angered by all this secrecy.

Annah was ushered to a chair with padded armrests; the same one used by the testing facility when they drew her blood. The female who was attending to her, tied a hollow rubber tube around her upper arm and quickly produced a test-tube shaped container. After rubbing the crease of her inner arm with an alcohol-doused gauze pad, a needle was gently inserted. Annah wanted to ask so many questions, but knew the language barrier hindered anything meaningful. Seconds later, the phlebotomist quickly made her exit with the sample, and Annah was left alone once again.

She waited, impatiently, for someone to come in with an explanation, but for several minutes she sat alone and uncertain. The deafening silence was broken by an exuberant celebration from the other room. There were cheers, laughter, and rejoicing. One of the male voices rose above the others and in very broken English shouted, "It's a perfect match!"

...I had hoped if they were celebrating with champagne, they would have at least offered me a glass. A dose of alcohol to settle my nerves would have been more than welcome. In the absence of any time keeping device to accurately account for the time lapse, I would guess I had been left alone for about half an hour. Finally the team was led out by a man, who I'm guessing was the head chemist or team leader. He motioned to me, with a subtle gesture, to follow the group into what I'd describe as a break room, or lounge.

There were two leather side chairs, a sofa, and several metal folding chairs randomly set up in no particular formation. Annah chose to sit in the oversized sofa that seemed to be the focal point of the room. Once the room filled, she was accompanied on the sofa by a tall lanky man. Grinning childishly and barely managing to bottle his excitement, he began to offer an explanation.

"A few years back we were offered an opportunity of a lifetime. I was asked to assemble a team of the highest caliber—a dream team of genetic scientists. We were contracted to conduct a DNA fingerprinting of a mummified skeleton found in the ruins of a cave near the banks of the Dead Sea. This cave was below where the Temple of Solomon once stood. There were flecks of preserved skin still attached to some of the bones and several strands of hair that we were able to collect for testing.

"DNA fingerprinting is a unique technique that uses a sequence referred to as micro satellite. These are small strings that tend to repeat several times in a person's DNA structure, and most of these shorter pieces are unique identifiers that are consistent in an individual's bloodline. Therefore, this type of testing is virtually foolproof for genealogical identification.

"Essentially, by using this method we were able to match the DNA sequences from these remains directly to you. We had visited you in your sleep several times to collect samples of blood, hair, skin, etc., but we could not get conclusive results because the conditions were not sterile. Eventually, we were forced to send a team to the testing lab where they posed as phlebotomists from the government on a top secret mission, allowing us to inconspicuously collect your sample."

Annah felt compelled to ask, "How were you certain I was the one?"

"Because the remains we found in the cave were that of a woman named Sophia, the Mother Goddess of all creation and through a thorough investigation we found that you carry the bloodline of the supreme goddess."

...To say I was in shock would have been an understatement. I had a million questions, but when I opened my mouth to speak, no words came out, just stuttering and stammering—an embarrassing commotion of indecipherable sounds. All eyes were on me, waiting for a reaction. But I couldn't seem to settle my thoughts long enough to formulate one coherent question. The whole concept, or idea, of being a scion to a supreme and divine individual was unfathomable. My friends and family won't believe it. It's not like I could go up to someone and introduce myself as a goddess or strategically note it on my resume. I want to believe that all of this is true, but my logical mind is erring on the side of an overactive imagination fueling a very creative delusion.

Annah looked around the room for hidden cameras, waiting for someone to jump out and inform her that this was a prank for a new TV reality show. Her knee-jerk reaction was to laugh hysterically, inviting the others to join in. They didn't seem at all amused by her over the top dramatic display. They were either good actors or what they told her was really true.

"Are you kidding me, DoctorWoj-cie-chow-ski?" She tried her best to pronounce his name, referencing the engraved tag pinned to his lab coat.

"You honestly expect me to believe this nonsense?"

"Of goddess descent?"

"This is ridiculous."

"Can I leave now?"

"You cannot return to your normal life, at least not until…" He was abruptly interrupted by a tall slender, middle-aged woman who had entered the room just minutes earlier. Her name was Magdalena.

"May I have a moment alone with her?" she asked in a gentle but authoritative tone.

The kind doctor excused himself and left the room.

"Would you like some coffee, tea, water?"

"Yes, that would be wonderful—coffee please."

Annah felt a measurable amount of angst diffuse, mainly because Magdalena had a better command of the English language, and somehow knew Annah needed a more subtle, empathetic approach. When she returned with the coffee, she sat next to Annah and began to explain the nature of their research, why her travels brought her to Wroclaw, and the complexity of the situation.

"We have been working on this project for quite some time now, so this victory is met with great exuberance. I understand this is a lot for you to absorb, and that it all seems ridiculous and inconceivable, but I can assure you, it is very real. As the doctor began to explain, Sophia is the Mother of the Universe; the Holy Spirit; the source of universal wisdom, the keeper of knowledge, the soul of all that is righteous and just.

"You may have heard of the Dead Sea scrolls that were recently found scattered among several Qumran Caves by the water's edge of the Dead Sea. Well, we found a handful of scrolls and stone tablets near Sophia's remains, deep inside one of the caves. We confiscated only her scrolls so they didn't fall into the wrong hands. If they had been found by the Pindar, leader of the illuminati, we probably wouldn't know what we know now.

"One particular fragment was encrypted, not written in Hebrew like the others. Our cryptologists, also an elite group, were able to decipher her encoded messages. Hopefully this epistle will shed some light."

I walk among you. You (mankind) don't know I'm there. I am Sophia. For thousands of years I have waited silently to reveal myself. Now is the time. Humanity is suffering because it has tangled itself into a knot so convoluted it can no longer see the forest for the trees. Speculation of how the world is going to end surrounds your every thought. Theories and predictions have you worried. It is now time to unveil the truth of the world's beginning and, without supreme intervention, its ultimate doom. Only you can educate the population to circumvent the impending Armageddon. Without your truth and power, the future of humanity's fate is sealed in cataclysm. You have always had the power. It is how you choose to wield it that will determine your success. It is not too late. But you must believe. Believe in yourself and humanity.

Your only enemy is the anti-Christ, who also walks with you. It is not a person. It is your alter-ego. You are born with both entities, good and evil. You choose which entity will prevail. For most, it is much easier to walk in a daunted existence then to choose to do the right thing. Society plays a huge part in which path you choose in your life's journey. You have become greedy, wasteful and selfish. Power struggles have become the mainstay. Luxury and material goods have become your way of life. You need to find a way to peacefully co-exist with each other or the world will end in devastation.

The benevolent gods are angry and growing weary because they cannot fight this battle alone any more. The deviant behavior of humanity is feeding the fire of the maleficent energies and they are growing stronger and more powerful. You need to decide if it is time to let the world end or to salvage what can be rebuilt. Take heed of this warning and let your passion be your only weapon and truth be your guide.

"Once all of her scrolls were translated, we were able to learn many of her secrets, the privileged truth of the universe. Sophia was the wisdom that inspired all of creation. In all of her divinity, she created a male and female who birthed two sons, Jehovah and Ildabaoth. They were the only two she entrusted with the truth, the custodians of her wisdom.

"As the world evolved, Sophia came to love all humans equally, which caused the envious natures of the brothers to emerge. They selfishly wanted all of the dear goddesses' attention and became rebellious and abhorrent when she divided it equally among all of mankind. The brothers vowed to keep humans ignorant to the secrets of creation so that they were the only ones who possessed this knowledge, making them very powerful.

"With their infinite power, came greed. They sold the sacred secrets to a powerful group of men that promised them riches and noble titles. They were called, the

Illuminati; the secret society to which King Solomon was leader. When the king died, he made sure all the secrets were buried with him. So without leadership or organization, the society slowly dissolved.

"Several years later, a new order of the society excavated his tomb and moved the sacred writings to Sophia's secret burial ground. They wanted to make sure all traces of her existence were buried together, this way the male gender would remain the dominating societal force, and women would always be relegated to subservient roles.

"Another one of Sophia's deeply coveted secrets was that of the Holy Grail. According to legend, the Holy Grail was the chalice Jesus used at the Last Supper. The writings, however, reveal that the Holy Grail was indeed at the Last Supper, but it was not an inanimate object. The term 'Holy Grail' was an anagram for 'A Holy Girl' and that girl was Sophia. In earlier times, many of the educated, or those who had acquired a higher social status, found it empowering to send messages to one another through word play, like anagrams for instance. If a word or phrase was not to be disclosed to a commoner, it would just be rearranged, leaving the less dignified in the dark about important revelations.

"Even today, there are many synchronicities that go unnoticed by commoners. Take a close look at the campaign brochures, logo, and bumper stickers for the 2008 U.S. presidential election. They read, 'OBAMA/ BIDEN'. At first glance, we saw that a man surnamed Obama was running for president, with a man surnamed

Biden as his running mate. What is uncanny is that during their term in office, the founder of al-Qaeda, Osama Bin Laden (Os*AMA*/*BInlaDEN*), was captured and killed. Coincidence, or was it an omen all along?

"Okay, so let's get back to the subject at hand. With the brothers' acts of treason, Sophia became enraged and decided it was best that she abandon her divine role and live as a human amongst the commoners. Her intention was to enlighten the world with her infinite wisdom and knowledge, but only to those who sought the truth and were not tied to the avaricious, material world. Her honorable quest was soon shattered.

"Living as a poor and homeless peasant, Sophia was shunned and considered an outcast by the very humans she adored. She became a minority in a world of egregious, self-indulgent creatures of despicable habit, and watched as the hatred, greed, ignorance, and bitter violence slowly devoured the world she created and loved so dearly.

"Sophia exiled herself to a cave in Jerusalem, vowing to only protect those who had stayed true to her, should calamity strike. But over time, her disparaged soul was tempered by empathy. Having been detached for far too long, and with a renewed sense of hope, she decided to come out of hiding and make her presence known once again—hoping to save all of creation from an inevitable annihilation.

"Recalling her first abominable attempt to walk amongst her peers, she felt it would be best to conceal her identity this time around. She shed her physical body in the cave, along with inscriptions on a stone tablet, and anecdotes on scrolls. Among the stone etchings were notations such as, '039N575W09'. Our cryptologists transliterated this as coordinates of longitude and latitude (39.5 North, 75.09 West), which brought us to the exact address of where you lived in Philadelphia. Below the symbols were drawings: a female infant, two fish forming a circle; a diagonal spear and a human figure carrying a jug of water on its shoulder. Translated it means a baby girl, born on the cusp of Aquarius and Pisces. So we concluded that her spirit was reborn to a female on February 19th. Needless to say, that is your birthdate. Her intention was to find a human body of the purest soul, a newborn. This way she was assured purity; a soul that didn't possess prejudices, biases, hate or scorn.

"Many spiritual groups have attempted to trace the origin and history of Sophia, but with the lack of any substantial evidence, they always hit a dead end. So to this day, Sophia is considered to be a mere personification of wisdom."

"Would you like to take a break?"

"No, thank you. Please continue." Annah was captivated, but was still understandably skeptical.

"The only ones that know about you are angels that live among us as humans. They were always there through your life to protect you and the secret. You may have noticed through your life tragedy never struck and you were always healthy and happy. If you were ever in danger, the threat was magically taken away, without your knowing."

Annah smiled when she suddenly remembered a few instances that had her baffled then, and still to this day.

...I was in the third grade, attending an elementary school in a not so desirable part of the city. As with most of my classmates, on a typical school day, we would walk home from school. We'd start walking in clusters, eventually branching off and following our own routes home. I usually ended up walking alone once we reached the first corner, just past the school grounds. No one I knew from my class lived in my neighborhood.

The city streets were, and probably still are, tricky to navigate because of school-cutting thugs, random acts of violence, and bullies who would no doubt either end up in jail or belong to a gang one day. These young villains would wait on corners, alley ways and even behind unkempt hedging for innocent prey, like me, to pass by.

On one particular day, I was only a block from the school when I heard a small group of boys, talking just loud enough to attract my attention. They said that if they caught me, they would throw me to the ground, grope me and beat me up. How cool were they? Three or four boys against a nine year old girl! I can only hope if they ever think back on that day, they see what cowards they truly were.

I held the straps of my book bag tightly and kept a steady pace. They were close behind me, hiding like undercover agents on a covert mission. I knew not to cower, scream or burst into tears—that's exactly what they wanted. You become very street smart when you grow up in a metropolis—mainly for survival. I casually looked behind me to see if they lost interest, but they hadn't.

My heart was racing and panic set in. I made a split second decision to run like hell, and based on the galloping steps I heard behind me, the boys followed my cue and hastened their pursuit. They weren't gaining on me, but were definitely keeping up with my pace. I soon came to realize that I wouldn't make it home. I still had several blocks to go. So as soon as I found an opportunity, I changed course and veered off on a side street and headed back to the school.

I ran through the opening in the wrought iron fence, zigzagged through the metal swings and monkey bars, finally reaching the concrete steps leading up to the familiar charcoal-green double doors. I pulled on both handles and heard the not so welcoming clang of chains holding the handles together on the inside. Pure adrenaline, fed from fear alone, pushed me to run to the next door just yards away. Thank goodness, that door opened. I quickly ran inside, hoping my predators hadn't seen me. I knew there was probably at least one custodian still in the building, but I had to suppress my urge to scream out for help in case I was wrong. It would only have given up my position, a chance I wasn't willing to take.

I sat in wait for mere moments when I heard heavy and labored footsteps approach the door. Crouching in the corner, I could feel their presence just inches from me. The only thing that separated me from my impending doom was an unchained steel door. I closed my eyes and prayed I would not be found, or worst case scenario, beaten to a pulp. I could hear my heart pounding as clear as the second hand on a clock in an empty room. Even though it felt like hours, realistically it was only seconds later that I opened my eyes to realize, with great relief, that the only thing I could hear was the sound of silence.

I slowly stood and peeked out of the rectangular window of one of the doors. No one was around. I couldn't imagine where they had gone.

Opening the door ever so slightly confirmed the coast was clear. I took off like a bat out of hell and didn't slow down or stop until I reached my front door. Once I was safely inside, I thought about what had just happened—thinking I never should have gotten away unscathed.

Magdalena repositioned herself on the sofa and continued, "The breakup with Lance caused a trauma in your life, just as we anticipated. We coerced this emotional upheaval, hoping that because you're a sensitive soul, it would trigger the awakening of your third eye, or pineal gland. Your research on that subject was commendable by the way. I believe you are now well-versed on the Kundalini energies.

"You see, Sophia has always been deep inside of you, waiting for her birth, which could only happen once your third eye was awakened. As I know you have learned, this is not a physical sight organ, but has the ability to see into other worlds and is vital in decoding the cryptic messages that were encoded by the Gods and Goddesses since the beginning of time.

"When Sophia's spirit was reborn, her vital soul remained intact and became a part of you as well. The vital soul contains all memories, experiences, emotions, etc., from previous lives. This is why your personal reading resonated with you. We had sent you this offer as soon as the time was right. We did in fact monitor your emails, friends and conversations using the handle, 'Wroclaw', as our network name. Great job on your powers of observation!

"Subtle messages were being sent to you through your subconscious pushing you in the right direction on your journey. You hadn't a clue about any of this until the transit began. You are probably wondering why Sophia didn't just have you write messages to yourself. That would have been amazing, if it could have been done. Unfortunately, the subconscious cannot speak, let alone write in a language you would understand. Therefore signs were placed directly in your path. And so the challenge began.

"I know this is only a brief dissertation, but time does not allow a full disclosure. The downside of all this is that our research has been breached. We are not completely confident that our discoveries have not fallen into the wrong hands. About six months ago, many of our transcripts, documents and discoveries disappeared along with a fellow researcher. Our theory is that he sold us out to the Secret Society. If this is indeed true, they will do anything and everything to keep your identity hidden. As a result, your life may be in danger. This is why we are in the process of creating an android.

"Once you enter the final phase of the rebirth, the android will assume the roles of your everyday life, basically just for appearance sake. This will hopefully keep the Society off your trail and everything will go smoothly."

"Final phase?" Annah questioned. "What do you mean by final phase?"

This was all too much to take in at one time. Final phase to Annah meant something that was about to come to an end, death, cessation of life, an untimely passing. She was hoping her assumption was wrong.

"Do you remember the key you ordered and immediately discarded?"

"Why yes! At the time I felt it was evil and didn't want it in my possession."

Magdalena scratched her brow before continuing, "The key was instrumental in keeping the universe's collective evil energies locked up, so it was intentionally sent to you as the keeper of all that is good. When you threw the key away, it immediately fell into the wrong hands and the underworld energies were released. As a result, the evil forces began to run rampant, brandishing their new found strength and power on the world. Their devilish antics immediately began to recruit those with dark souls over to their camp. It is not a coincidence that we are currently experiencing unprecedented disasters and crippling financial hardship. Their power is only increasing and must be stopped. They need to be lured back to their underground world and locked away forever, with no chance for resurrection.

"You are going to have to battle and slay the keeper of the dark gates to entomb these energies. Therefore, you must prepare yourself for this ultimate battle. Just know it is your mind that needs to be conditioned. It will be your mental energy that prevails, and will ultimately be triumphant. Once you have accomplished this feat, all of Sophia's power will be bestowed upon you. You will be revered and your words of wisdom will ring though the land. You will be able to relate to modern society, specifically those who suffer from loss, betrayal and abandonment. Your role will be to enlighten the world, steering them away from disaster and a global demise."

With those final instructions...the room went dark.

FANTASY OR REALITY

*August 3*rd

Through the small slits in my waking eyes, I could see splashes of sunlight peeking in. I rolled my pillow over my face as I do most mornings when I'm not quite ready to greet the day. It felt as though I had just gone to bed. Why do the night hours fly by at mach speed, while days march to the rhythm of a negative cadence? I feel the same about weekends. No sooner do I tuck myself in on Friday night, I am waking up to a Monday morning…aka, start of a new work week. And this vicious cycle, unfortunately, is a ball and chain we drag around for life.

Annah managed to lift her heavy head off the pillow, stretching her arms high over her head to work out all the kinks her body had developed during the night. She threw her limp and lifeless legs over the side of the bed waiting for them to be fully functional before she attempted to stand. Once she was upright, she made the bed, gathered up the laundry, and brewed her morning breakfast blend. Every day—same chores—same order!

She watched the morning news while sipping her heavily creamed and sugared dose of caffeine, holding her cup up high to thank the gods for the blessings in her life. She embraced her newfound spirituality, an otherwise unfamiliar feeling that now felt uncannily natural. Overnight, she had become one with the world and everyone in it.

Annah's thoughts were buoyantly drawn to her most recent travels. Still in a state of awe, she couldn't help but imagine how her life would change once she assumed this enviable role. She even began to envision public reactions once this declaration was announced throughout the world.

Anxious to record her latest excursion in her journal, she nestled in the coziest nook in the house and immediately began to write the entire experience, verbatim, entering every intricate detail. She raced through several pages, writing savagely, fearing if she didn't write it all down in one sitting, a very important element may unintentionally be omitted.

When she finished her impromptu short-story, and gave it her blessing, she couldn't help but think of questions she wished she'd asked, specifically about the dangers of this venture and why she was allowed to leave with such a big threat hanging over her. The 'final phase' aspect still remained arbitrary and, unfortunately, left to her nimble-witted interpretation.

Without concrete answers, Annah wasn't sure what to think, what to do, or how to process all the recent activity and information. She was anxiously elated, but at the same time convincing herself that she had lost all sense of reality. Her mind was prompting her that this type of behavior was usually reserved for those taken away in a straightjacket, or someone heavily medicated to induce lethargy due to their mental incapacities. And just the fact that she was engaging in a dialogue with herself didn't help matters. Did she even have an ounce of sanity left to be able to distinguish between normal and irrational behavior?

Annah pulled out The Contract yet again. She now felt a connection to its message and could make better sense of its meaning; specifically its mention of a project that was still fermenting.

It is clear that this project comes from an idea, which exists deep inside of you. This idea is not yet mature and it is not yet the moment to reveal it, but the time will come. You should not worry too much about exactly how things will happen, events will occur quite naturally. I have also spoken to you about an encounter which will have a certain importance for you concerning this project. This encounter will even be the vital moment that kick-starts the evolution, so you should be very active and ready to seize any opportunity which comes your way. Above all, it is important that you make yourself available to contact a great deal of people and pay attention to how and why you made these contacts.

With that being said, and while her daughters were still sleeping, she felt it was the opportune time to try and validate some of the most recent events. She had no idea where to start, especially if all knowledge of Sophia was kept secret by the Society. Even more importantly, would she be able to trust anything she found on the internet?

Sharing her experiences on social media was definitely out of the question. No one in their right frame of mind would believe such an outlandish story. Besides, just in case there was a hint of truth in what she was told by Magdalena, she would run the risk of the Society finding her. Quite honestly though, she felt it was an honor if all this were true, but at the same time wished it had been bestowed upon someone else.

Annah decided she was ready to further explore the messages that were bequeathed to her. The internet actually had more links about Sophia than she had imagined it would. For the most part, a lot of what she was told was confirmed and, in some cases, expanded on; which now had her wondering if what she was told actually came from one of these websites.

The most interesting point, and also a recurring theme on every site, was that Sophia's existence followed a very distinct pattern—her birth, her exile and inevitably, her return. The only inconsistent argument was whether she lived a full life before she shed her physical body to be reborn.

If this theory were true, will she be with Annah until the day she dies?

Annah began to recall certain excerpts from her conversation at Wroclaw. One particular point that stood out and reverberated as the most prominent of the consultation was that her mind needed to be conditioned. It was her mental energy that would become the weapon of choice. Needless to say, the fact that the word 'weapon' was used was not very promising.

So what was she supposed to do next?

Sit around and wait for the stars to continue to guide her?

She was a bag of mixed emotions, fearing the impending danger, exalted by the notion that she would be carrying out such a worldly deed and exuberated by the adventure that was placed so carefully on her life's path.

But the question Annah was struggling with the most was, "Am I living in reality or have I concocted the most elaborate fantasy imaginable?"

THE ULTIMATE BATTLE

...It was only 7:30 in the morning, so I decided to use the next few hours to just sit and think. I went out to the back patio knowing it would pacify my erratic mood by just enjoying the calm serenity of the rising sun. Hearing the joyful chirping, and watching the playful fluttering of the early birds, brought me back to nature—back to the wonderful things to be appreciated without a price, filling me with a healthy dose of gratification. We honestly do take a lot for granted and should be more thankful for all of creation. My philosophical side came forward as I questioned why we are so hell bent sometimes to hurt one another, envy what we wished we had, and casually destroy the natural elements in the world.

The morning was unseasonably crisp for early August, like a refreshing sneak preview of autumn, Annah's favorite season. Its rejuvenating quality lifted her to a happy place, so she decided she wasn't going to sit around and wait for an invitation to get started. This was a day for forward movement and so out the door she went for her morning walk.

Annah was up to a little over a mile, daringly changing the route and pace every day to add variety. Depending on the time she ventured out, she would either encounter the one neighbor rushing to get the kids off to daycare before work, the one whose lawn sprinklers were carefully placed the night before, so they only had to turn on the spigot in the morning to start the oscillation process, or the one who made a mad dash for the morning paper, sometimes in nothing more than his boxers and t-shirt. She felt blessed that she had gotten to the point of not being intimidated by what others were thinking, or worrying about those uncomfortable glares she always felt were mischievously directed at her.

When she got home, she opened all the windows in the house. She wanted to break the claustrophobic monotony of being boxed in all summer. After her shower, she made a quick trip to the market to pick up the ingredients for one of her most requested meals—Hawaiian chicken over angel hair pasta, hoping her daughters hadn't already made plans for dinner. She missed her girls over the past few weeks and they needed to see that Mom was slowly returning to her normal self.

...By the time I got home from the market, the house was fully awake. I was even greeted at the door. The grocery bags were taken in, unloaded and everything was put away. Without them saying a word, I could feel their elation that we were going to have a dinner together, just like we used to.

Annah spent the better part of the afternoon on her finances, reconciling her bank accounts and paying her bills. Some of the bills, which she is embarrassed to admit, had fallen due and now were several weeks late. Never in her life had she missed a payment. This was a major reality check that she needed to get back to the game of life—and soon.

At dinner, the conversation was limited to playing catch up, mainly because Annah still didn't feel comfortable discussing the extracurricular goings on in her life—a topic she still hadn't decided if she'd ever reveal to them. Some things are better left unsaid...especially since the overall census was that she was finally embracing life again.

After dinner, the dishes were cleared and the kitchen cleaned up. Annah let her daughters know it was okay if they wanted to go out and hang out with their friends. There was no sense in them sitting around just to keep her company, and besides, she was exhausted and probably would go to bed early anyway.

Annah made it through about half of the movie, *Forrest Gump*, when her eyelids repeatedly rolled over her sagging eyes. Knowing it was just a matter of time before they sealed shut, it was time to call it a night. She changed into her favorite nightshirt and decided to do something she hadn't done since she was little. Kneeling down next to her bed, she recited a bedtime prayer she had written earlier in the day. She called it, "Sophia's Prayer."

As I put myself to sleep,
I trust that I will not tremble or weep;
The universe in all its' mystique,
Will whisper the wisdom I truly seek;
Allow me, to see the light,
That shines so brilliantly and oh so bright;
Please help me through the night and day,
Continue to guide me by leading the way;
You've granted me the strength I seek,
I am now a warrior that isn't so weak;
Thank you Sophia for all that you've done,
I love the person that I have become.
Amen.

When Annah reached over to turn off the light, she knew that once darkness filled the room, it was only a matter of time before she was taken far away. Her eyes had barely shut when she found herself staring down at her body, so subdued, peaceful and calm, not knowing what the night would bring or even if she'd be returning to it by daybreak.

Something felt so final about that night.

She was transferred through the ether, entranced by the beauty of the voluminous sky, the bright full moon with its freckles of lavender, and by the stars that speckled the infinite black canvas. The stars began to tumble about like the shiny beads in a kaleidoscope, slowly forming a vortex that slowly pulled her in. At the tapered end of the cyclonic twister was a glaring white light. She created a visor with her hands to deflect the blinding effects of the intense flare.

...Could it have been the proverbial white light we supposedly gravitate towards on our final voyage home? I struggled to stop my forward movement, but my efforts were met with great resistance. Control of my body had already been relinquished to a higher power. All I could do was close my eyes and allow the universe to take the reins. This supposed passage through heaven's gate was a feeling like no other, a whisper of warm breath wafted over my face and body, arousing a myriad of titillating sensations—liberation, exhilaration, and a passionate love of life. Unclothed and vulnerable, and totally cleansed of pride, prejudice and pretentiousness, I felt like a pioneering spirit that had been reborn—given new life.

Annah made landfall, and by carefully assessing the landscape around her, established that she was once again in Jerusalem. Ahead of her was Solomon's temple, and just over the drop off were the Qumran caves where Sophia's remains and scrolls were found.

A sheer white frock appeared on the ground by her feet that she immediately slipped into. Although frumpy and shapeless, the drafty air caused the clumsily draped material to flatten, exposing the profile of her flawless, shapely body that stood so innocent and unassuming. The perfect tendrils of her waist length hair floated behind her like rose petals riding the tiny ripples of the wind. She was poised, graceful and alluring—all the qualities of the ravishing goddess she was destined to become.

The murmurs of an amassing crowd grew louder and stronger as they encroached on the roughly stacked boulders about a quarter mile behind her. The clamor steadily heightened as the assemblage declared their prime parcels in preparation for a production that was undoubtedly scheduled to begin momentarily.

There were thousands of these on-lookers that eventually lined the entire row of rocks, packing in maybe ten to twelve rows deep. She turned in their direction, giving an affirming smile. They gratified her gesture by cheering and chanting a phrase she couldn't make out because all the voices melded into one melodious hum.

Each spectator carried a tall torch made of straw and twigs. When the conglomeration of flickering lights was brought together, the sky lit up like the sun on the horizon, about to present itself for the day. It was also bright enough to allow Annah to maneuver without stumbling or falling. She instinctively knew to move forward, and although glancing back several times, she also knew retreating was not an option.

The temple grew grander and more intimidating as she approached its gates. She entered the courtyard and sauntered over the marble walk and up the steps to the doors that, once again, opened to let her in. Even with the sense of familiarity, she had an uneasy feeling that something was eerily different.

Annah walked through the foyer and made her way down the center aisle, inspecting every corner, statue, and pew. The tiny hairs on her body raised; she feared something was lurking in the dimly lit shadows. Her imagination had definitely piqued. She could have sworn one of the statues turned its head, but hoped it was just an illusion or play of lights.

She walked up to the same door, behind the pulpit, that was locked on her last visit. This time it slowly creaked open allowing her to enter. There were five steps just inside the door, leading to a lower level. She grabbed one of two flaming torches that was embedded in a large fissure in the stone wall, and crouched down to see as far down the narrow passage as she could—before she descended into the abysm of darkness.

From about the third step down, she was met with an unpleasant odor, not completely identifiable—a possible hybrid of feces, decomposing carcasses, or maybe even maggot infested garbage. Whatever its origin, it was unbearable. She felt light-headed and queasy. With the torch extended an arm's length ahead, she was able to see a twisting narrow tunnel; beyond that, it was pitch-black. With short, intentional steps, she tentatively pressed on.

There were a handful of doors along the way, hidden in recessed alcoves. She pushed one of them open and stepped inside. The room glittered with the treasures of a thousand kings; some stacks were ceiling high. Treasure chests overflowed with sparkling jewels, dazzling gems and glittering gold coins. Gold bars were neatly arranged in one corner, surrounded by rich tapestry and spools of gold thread. She wanted to sit one of the slovenly stacked coin piles and toss them playfully in the air, but she was impelled to move on, as if the greatest treasure was waiting for her at the end of the passage.

The tunnel, which didn't have defined dimensions, began to taper to half its original width and height. It was either an illusion induced by the contaminated and thin air she was breathing, or the tunnel was closing in on her. She kept her wits about her though and ploughed through, like Joan of Arc leading her troops into battle.

The glow from Annah's torch generated a bright reflection several feet ahead. Squinting to make out its origin, Annah saw a heavy wooden door secured to the cinder stone by sturdy brass hinges. She had reached the end of the tunnel. With anxious hesitation, she grabbed the door handle, and while depressing the lever with her thumb, tried to push the door open. It wouldn't budge, even when she pressed the weight of her body against it. A part of her was relieved, while another part was questioning why she was brought all that way for nothing.

She released the lever and took several steps back. A small ray of light emanated from the keyhole, which was very small in comparison to the dimension of the door. In fact, the keyhole would only accommodate one type of key and based on the size and shape, it was the key that was sent to Annah; the one she no longer had. The feeling of defeat was overwhelming. She fell to the floor sobbing and gasping for air. The disappointment was more than she could bear. She had done so much and come so far, and now, because of one misstep, one single mistake that she will probably regret forever, her journey was over.

...I begged the universe for another chance, pleading and asking, "What had I done in life that was so dreadfully wrong that I deserved this?" I didn't get an answer, not that I expected one. I guess my thought process was that if I verbalized my angst, it

would be somewhat of a consolation for me. Feeling sorry for myself, however, was just prolonging the inevitable. I had to shamefully confront the crowd that had gathered to show their faith and support in something that, because of my negligence, will never come to pass.

Annah turned to leave, but was paralyzed by a gruesome sound coming from inside the locked room. It was horrifying. What she heard wasn't human or recognizable as any animal, domestic or wild. To best describe it, she would have to say it sounded like a mutated combination of hissing, gnarling, snarling, gurgling, and raspy howling.

…Had I reached the devil's gate? Was the beast on the other side of the door the keeper of the underworld? Frightened to the point of desperation, my only recourse was to find my way outside, to safer ground, and think through what I was going to do next. I left the burning torch at the door and frantically scrambled back through the twisting and turning narrows.

The snarling beast grew angrier; its intensified bellows reverberated through the tunnel, bouncing off the walls, causing the mortar to crumble, and rocks to tumble in the path behind Annah. The powder that aggressively filled the tunnel had her gasping for breathable air. The crackles of disintegrating stone were soon replaced by the plunging and pounding of granite slabs from the floors above.

Rubbing the sweat from her eyes, she saw that she was only feet away from the entrance; she had made it safely. She could hear faint cheers, and see flickers of the fiery torches that lined the distant rock border. Having run several yards beyond the compound, she felt to the ground from exhaustion.

She closed her eyes and begged that this nightmare be over, that she be returned to her bed, to wake up in her world, her reality. Unfortunately, her pleas were ignored. She could hear the hecklers in the distance and listened intently to their intonation. They were incessantly chanting, "SO-PHI-A, SO-PHI-A, SO-PHI-A." But Annah knew she had failed as their beloved goddess; a role that she now felt never should have been bestowed upon her in the first place.

...They think I am goddess Sophia. Somewhere, in the course of this travel, I was reborn. What Magdalena told me must have been true, and this must be the final phase she spoke of. Now I have no choice but to continue on, for the sake of humanity. But where do I go from here? What do I do?

Annah turned to what used to be the beautiful fortress of Solomon's Temple, crumbled to the ground, reduced to ruins; unable to understand what was left for her to do. She hadn't accomplished anything, and wasn't crowned as she understood from The Contract. This was nothing short of an epic failure.

The crowd lowered their chants to a dull clamor, as if the finale of fireworks had just fizzled out in the sky. There she stood, ashamed, confused and disheartened, stripped of her dignity, reduced to what she always was and probably always will be—an average face in the crowd—accredited with nothing more than an unpolished moment to shine.

As she watched the spectators disband, the tears she had courageously fought off began to pour down her face and spatter into a small puddle that hadn't dried up from the last rain. She reached down, cupping the fresh cool water in her hands to douse her dingy, sweaty face. When she reached for her second handful, the puddle began to ripple; the earth beneath her quavered with short, precise, measured movements.

The glow of torches in the distance, from those who were returning to their homes, suddenly stood still as the tremors increased in intensity and volume. Like a herd of wildebeest running aimlessly across the African veldt, the dispirited masses began to stampede back to their vacated positions, behind the rocks. They appeared more confident that the show would still go on and that Annah was still the star.

...I was concerned that no one in the crowd seemed concerned or fearful of the unsteadiness of the earth, or the grisly bellows of a beast that had yet to reveal itself. I, on the other hand, was preparing myself to behold a creature that would undoubtedly breakdown my bravado.

Not once did Annah look in the crowd's direction, but she could feel the stares penetrating her body like lasers. In fact, she was drawing energy from it. Something deep inside her was whispering inspiration to her soul and a blanket of protection shrouded her like invisible armor. She recalled the edifying words by the researcher at Wroclaw, assuring her that her conditioned mental energy will prevail and triumph.

An invisible force nudged her to walk towards the crumbled and still settling fortress. White billows infused the sky with dust and powder like the weightless puffs of smoke from a doused fire. Stopping within fifty feet of the sunken mount, she found the fallen sanctum visually hard to digest.

A beaming light shot up from the deep depression and played on the dark sky like a beacon guiding lost ships on a foggy night. It was like a metaphor that Annah was able to translate to the recent events in her life, a defining moment. Up to that point, the meaning of her life had been unclear and in desperate need of guidance. It was time to dissipate the metaphorical fog by letting go of outmoded thoughts, to dispose of all the emotional baggage that was no longer useful, to purge the indiscretions she had dismissed as flagrant mistakes over the years, and to dismantle her arsenal of dishonorable acts and intentions—releasing them to the universe once and for all. Once this ritual of absolution was complete, she felt an unequivocal passionate feeling of love and resolve.

...My moment of amnesty was short lived however. A wicked dynamism filled the air and my immediate surroundings became noxiously unstable. I could sense fear from the spectators behind me, but I didn't let it discourage, dispirit or weaken me in any way.

From the rubble, Annah's worst fear began to emerge in the form of a despicable abomination that only the devil could have created, a hideous bastard of all that evil represents—her formidable opponent.

It grabbed the earth with its long pointed claws. Its tapered tail swept the sandy soil creating a trench in its wake; its smooth, shiny scales glimmered in the moonlight, its yellow marble eyes were symmetrically divided by a black slit and its slithery, long black tongue was forked at the end. Two serpentine heads branched out from its neck, writhing independently of each other. She watched cautiously as it stretched its body from the confines of the prison it had been housed in for thousands of years.

The fire that surged from its fanged mouth hurled a spark that landed dreadfully close to Annah's feet. She extinguished the cinder and noticed, lying on the ground by her feet, a wooden spear topped with a gold pointed tip and a gold embossed shield. She hadn't a clue where it came from, but was appreciative of the fact that she now had some sort of defense. Now, with these armaments in hand, she felt and looked like a warrior goddess.

The creature, still adjusting to its surroundings, turned in Annah's direction. Its body remained anchored while the two heads slithered towards her, using their sensory tongues to determine if Annah was a predator or prey. It came relatively close, then suddenly backed off and reared its heads high; probably to analyze the chemical particles it picked up from her.

Annah held tight to the spear in her right hand and even tighter to the shield in her left. While waiting for the beast to decide her fate, she thought back to Magdalena's conversation at Wroclaw, specifically the part about the 'final phase'. Now that she was in the heat of the moment, she knew this battle could go either way. She also knew, if she didn't make it out, an android was waiting to take her place in the real world, which for her, wasn't an option. She wasn't going to let that heartless, computerized, humanoid machine raise her children, or take over her life. If only she knew how this was going to play out, she could make an informed decision to end the journey now. But what would the repercussions be? Would it adversely affect humanity?

The creature slithered in again. Annah decided to stand her ground, bravely releasing her inhibitions and fear, finding strength from the familiar adage, "face your fears." She stood tall, and waited for the creature to make its move. Her heart was racing; the anticipation was unbearable.

What was it waiting for?

"Come and get me you hideous monster!" she screamed.

She held her spear up, hoping to antagonize the beast. It snarled loudly and gazed down at Annah. She stared back, knowing in a matter of minutes it would all be over. The dueling heads came forward and circled around her, trying to smell her fear.

She knew she was no match for it physically and was already told her mental energy would be her weapon of choice. She rallied all her internal strength; all the wisdom she had gained all the inspiration she had gathered, and glowered into its eyes.

...I had read somewhere that if you follow a spiritual life for a sufficient time your chakras will perfectly align, from the base of your spine to your crown (the top of your head). Chakras are the center of spiritual power in the human body. Once aligned you are able to connect with higher realms and experience an inner strength that you never thought possible. It wasn't until that moment, in the shadow of the beast, that I realized The Contract mentioned my efforts would be crowned. Foolishly, I thought this meant I was getting a tiara, or a diamond studded head piece; now in all my wisdom, I understand the crowning to mean I am spiritually centered and can use this internal power to fuel my strength and defeat the evils of the world.

Now armed with the knowledge of her spiritual enlightenment, and having attained her crown chakra, she had the strength and confidence to do what needed to be done. Through mental telepathy, she communicated with the creature. Annah knew from a number of psychology books she had read, we are our own worst enemy. We feed on what we are told and most times manifest our insecurities that imprison us in our self-imposed fears. If you think back to when you were little, it wasn't until you heard of or watched movies about monsters that you started to imagine they were under the bed or hiding in the closet. And when you got older, immediately after watching a horror movie or reading a suspense thriller, you began to imagine things hiding in the shadows or behind the shower curtain; or you'd hear strange noises when you were alone, believing your house is haunted. These thoughts only surfaced because of something you heard or read; we involuntarily allow our minds to play tricks on us.

With that in mind, she knew by sending subliminal, telepathic suggestions, she could mentally cripple the beast into submission. It would relinquish its power and submit to Annah's will. She closed her eyes and forced her thoughts into its mind, watching as it became paralyzed, mesmerized, frozen in time.

She tested its lethargic state by walking closer, albeit with great hesitance and justifiable reserve. It still didn't move. Standing directly in front of where its heads divided, she was about to wield her spear into the torso of its massive body, to pierce its heart through its scaly hide. But her new found wisdom reminded her that something so evil could not be slain by debilitating a heart that was cold and lifeless to begin with. She had to destroy its dark soul.

Remembering back to the research she'd done, one single element came forward and replaced all her thoughts—*the eyes are the window to the soul.*

At that moment, she knew exactly what she had to do. Beckoning for the slithering heads to come closer, and with deliberate intention, she thrust her spear into its eye. It violently thrashed about, eventually crashing to the ground with a thunderous bang. It wailed a horrific series of cries and took several laboring breaths.

After several minutes, no sound was heard or movements made.

The beast was dead.

Annah turned to the crowd, holding the shield to her side. They cheered so loudly it echoed for miles. Tears of joy streamed down her face as she watched the enormous carcass sink into the abyss that opened in the middle of the crumbled fortress. The beast was now entombed in the depths of hell. The challenge was over and Annah had won. She now felt worthy of being their goddess, Goddess Sophia.

THE MORNING AFTER

Annah was anxious to relate everything that happened to Doctor Oliver, so she brought her journal to her appointment. He listened intently, as usual, stopping only to take a few notes. When she was done he was quick to respond, "Each trip offered a thread for you to move along on your journey, causing you to believe you had to piece a puzzle together. Overall, because of these distractions, you weren't thinking about your heartache and were actually traveling on a road to recovery by thinking you had to solve this mystery.

"With each trip you believed the takeaway provided clues alluding to the fact that you were a goddess onto yourself. But you were able to figure that out on your own. You had to beat this illness with your own strength and wisdom. The battle was in your dreams because you had to face your worst fear and overcome it. You faced your darkness and were victorious. You, my dear, beat the demon called depression."

"Wow," she whispered with a confident and affirming grin.

"But I believe your greatest test is still to come."

*August 4*th

"There is an air of finality today. I know my travels are over, there's nothing left for me to do in the astral world. But because I indulged in The Contract, followed through on my challenge, my life has changed forever. I unknowingly and involuntarily followed a trail of significantly vivid dreams, prodding me to make choices, using wisdom as my compass. If you had asked me a month ago what my life's purpose was, I wouldn't have been able to tell you. Now I know. It is to transfer my mystical knowledge, inherent power, and acquired courage to the real world. I am to face the beasts on the mortal plane head on, using this experience as a cornerstone. Obviously, I will not be slaying a two-headed beast or slinking through ancient pyramids, but I know I will be confronted by diversity, malevolence, and there will be several puzzling circumstances crossing my path. Whatever life decides to throw at me, I'll have the wisdom and courage to overcome it."

Annah knew that even though the challenge was over, there was still something rather important to address. She had to prepare for her encounter with Lance and somewhere in the fray, prepare for her return to work. It was time to refer to The Contract, once again, to refresh her memory. The dates for which the encounter was to take place were between the thirteenth and eighteenth, giving her a little over a week to work out all the details, from planning her call to setting up a specific activity. Noticeably, she was far calmer than she was weeks ago, and commendably demure. Over the course of the past few weeks, she had grown emotionally, without any great effort on her part. Smiles replaced tears, and optimism replaced despair. She was now in a place where dreams were possible and setbacks were just lessons in disguise.

"...I will plan the call for August 13th. That's a Sunday, which is perfect. His attention won't be hindered by work or anything else that would cause an unfocused conversation. Hopefully, it will create a relaxed and jovial climate. The last thing I would want is to be rushed or have him feel preoccupied in any way. As far as proposing a fun activity, we had done so much together already, creating a new and exciting atmosphere proved challenging, even for my creative mind. I don't want to make him feel pressured or have reservations that the date may end on an intimate note. I will propose to meet at a local coffee shop for lattes and pastry. Not exciting, but not intimidating either. I may or may not tweak this plan in the upcoming days, but at least I have something in place."

Annah finished up her exercise tape, took a leisurely stroll through the neighborhood, and followed it all up with a steamy, relaxing shower. Still wrapped in her terry towel, she sprawled across the bed and gave in to the alluring call of a calming slumber. Moments into her restful escape, she was awakened by a rapping on her bedroom door. Laughing to herself, she thought back to her frightful encounters of being woken up by entities and illustrious dreams.

The door slowly opened.

"Mom?" asked a soft voice.

"Are you awake?"

Annah answered in a playful, sarcastic tone, "Not really, but come in."

"I'm not sure if you want to hear this, but I'd rather you hear it from me than someone else."

Annah's daughter seemed uncharacteristically somber.

"I just read on my friend's Myspace that Lance is engaged. I don't know if I upset you, but you *are* over him, right?"

"It's okay. I'm sure I would have heard about it eventually. Thanks for letting me know….love you."

"Love you, Mom!

The door quietly closed.

"…It's true that time heals all wounds. So very true! Boy, have the tables turned. I waited a month for a moment that will never come to pass. I know I'm stronger emotionally, but I still can't help but wonder what would have happened had I pursued him from the start; let him know that I wanted him back and still loved him very deeply. If I hadn't listened to The Contract, how would this have played out? I guess if it was meant to be, it would've been. It is what it is! I am ready to move on to greener pastures and live by the words I have come to appreciate…there are no mistakes in life, just lessons to be learned!"

This journey, for Annah, was remarkable from start to finish. At first, she wouldn't have wished it on her worst enemy, but after going through the process, she believes that anyone who loses their way, or questions their purpose would benefit from the experience.

"...At this point, you would think this is the end, but for me it's just the beginning!"

THE END.